MUKTANANDA

MUKTANANDA
Selected Essays

edited by

PAUL ZWEIG

Harper & Row, Publishers

New York, Hagerstown, San Francisco, London

Afterword from Muktananda Siddha Guru by Shankar reprinted by permission of
S.Y.D.A. Foundation

Designed by Janice Stern

Library of Congress Cataloging in Publication Data

Muktananda Paramhamsa, Swami.
   Selected essays.
   1. Spiritual life (Hinduism)—Addresses, essays, lectures. I. Title.
BL1228.M825 1976   294.5′4   76–9994
ISBN 0–06–069860–8

---

78 79 80 10 9 8 7 6 5 4 3 2

Just as pearls on a necklace are strung on one string, likewise all the individual souls are strung on the same thread, which is God.

Swami Muktananda

Contents

Introduction
by Paul Zweig

Since meeting Swami Muktananda during his recent tour of the United States, I have heard him speak on dozens of occasions. I have watched his extraordinarily mobile face reflect compassion, interest or anger, while never losing its steadiness and impregnability. Everything about him seemed bathed in certainty, like a marvelous actor in the play of life or, at the opposite extreme, like a man whose spontaneity never lapses. Eventually I understood that these qualities, which make even his light moods stark and intense, constitute the very definition of a Sadguru, a "fully realised" spiritual master. They are not personal traits which he happens to possess, but the result of prolonged, single-minded training under the guidance of his own Guru, the Siddha master, Swami Nityananda.

In India, people often travel great distances simply to greet a Sadguru. They sit attentively in the same room with him, or just receive his blessing and go. The teaching they have come for doesn't take the form of wise sayings, or of moral advice which they might have obtained by listening to a friend. What they come to learn is the example of the man himself. They want to know with their own eyes that the highest teaching of the spiritual tradition has been embodied in the riveting presence of a human being, a saint who they can talk to and see, and touch.

From the moment I met him, Swami Muktananda overturned

all my ideas about the spiritual life. His very presence seemed to cry out that there was no spiritual life separate from a worldly life; that the activities of one's normal existence, the pains and pleasures, tragedies and successes, were the one field which every man ploughed and reaped according to his acts. The field was spiritual or worldly as one chose to make it. And the difference was intangible. It was a matter of seeing it so. Why live in a monastery or a cave, insists Swami Muktananda, why shuck off the commitments of normal living, substituting a special category of "pious" looks for the full range of acts and feelings which arise within us, when the loveliness of the Self pulsates wherever and whenever we see it.

Swami Muktananda—Baba, as his disciples call him—says over and over: "God dwells within you as you"; not as some privileged and better part of you, not as some extra oriental sense added on to the five we know, but as all of you: the angers, the traits of character, the tastes and preferences, the skills and also the lack of skills. God is not someone you have to learn how to become; He is you, as you.

Merely to consider this idea required that I set aside my familiar assumptions about human personality and about God. I had to stop thinking of myself as a complicated sort of failure made up of "normal" neuroses and anxiety, shaped by high ideals which merely disguised low animal cravings. I also had to stop imagining God as some better human personality enthroned in a distant place, some cosmic autocrat who ran a flawed though sometimes splendid show in which human beings were the clowns or, more precisely, the gladiators who always lost. To tell the truth, until I met Baba, and was stunned by the emotional avalanche which his mere presence broke loose in me, I never knew what I meant when I wrote or thought about God. The word would impose itself with a feeling of transparency, of courage even, yet I had no religious affiliation. On the contrary, I felt that the institutional religions I knew, along with their somewhat pompous ceremonies, were oppressive, unliberating, and generally intolerant. I preferred my own free-style God, and my own casual spirituality to which I gave little thought and from which I got little pleasure, aside from the convenient literary one of inserting "God,"—whatever that meant—in a poem or essay.

Swami Muktananda put it differently. God is a way of being human, he said. God is the interior sky across which the clouds of particular thoughts and feelings drift and disappear. God, to use one of Baba's favorite Christian sayings, is "the inner kingdom." He is the uniquely human faculty of self-awareness. He is not an idea, a person, an object of thought, but the faculty of thinking itself which Baba calls "the inner witness." God is the activity I must perform all the time in order to be me. He is not ideal and far away. He is not making a list of my failures to punish me later. He is not interested in my feelings of guilt and expiation. He is so close to me that there is no way to tell us apart.

If only we could experience ourselves with complete self-acceptance from the standpoint of this "inner witness," or God, or Self, Baba says, there would be nothing more to learn. We would be liberated in a snap of the fingers from the anxiety of human limitations. We would know ourselves as a hub of the flow of existence, and the world would be ours.

Although Swami Muktananda is a charming storyteller, with a gift for simplifying the most abstruse philosophical propositions, the centerpiece of his lesson is not an idea or a logical demonstration. He is himself the lesson. For a Sadguru, a master of Siddha Yoga, is characterised by this: he has abolished every difference between what he is and what he says. To properly absorb his teaching, therefore, it is not enough to hear him speak, one must absorb his very presence by learning oneself to become equally present.

A "fully realised" master has arrived at a state of complete mental self-possession. He has recast his personal identity, by anchoring it wholly and permanently at the inner apex of self-awareness. He has done this by means of continuous training, in the form of meditation. Above all, he has focused his attention, perhaps for years, on his own Guru, taking to himself all the aspects of his Guru's "fully realised" humanity. He has surpassed his personal ego, by replacing it with the steadiness and needless-ness of his master, to whom he has surrendered his thoughts. By means of this unique relationship, he has levered himself into a new awareness of his identity, replacing the defensive ego with the unchanging "inner witness" or Self, or God. And that is what he demands of us: the same act of self-surrender. For a Sadguru has only one interest: to liberate his disciple even from discipleship, by making him into another Sadguru.

For a Westerner, this is the sticking point. How can I accept such an offer when all my efforts since childhood have pulled me in an opposite direction. All my life, it seems, I have been trying to "grow up," to become my own person by fencing off my individuality, posting guards of suspicion and emotional distance. "I want to be me," goes a popular song, not him or her or them. We are convinced that individuality requires distance; that knowing "who we are," means knowing who we are not. To stand at all, we have to stand alone. And if we are sad, lonely, if our experiences of love are fleeting and inadequate, that is a price we pay grumblingly for the honor of being someone. We say: that's life, let's be realistic. If we're tradition-minded, we invoke original sin. If we're modern, we think of civilisation and its Freudian discontents which we experience in our own inescapable sadness and accept, in return for the privilege of "adulthood."

In the face of this, Baba says: your goal—inner autonomy—is correct, but your method—defensive egotism—is wrong, because no matter how good you become at defending yourself, you'll never conquer your own vulnerability. You may stave off partial defeats at the hands of your fellow men, albeit at the cost of increasing mental rigidity and isolation, but old age and death have got to win no matter what you do.

A defender's ego is ruled by fear and an abiding suspicion of its underlying helplessness. But Baba says: "God is just on the other side of fear," and you can get to Him, by simply letting go. If you could stop defending yourself even for a moment, you would discover that your enemies had been your own creation all along. It is you who divided up the world, and when, for a moment, you give up that divisive view, you become reunited with the whole of your experience, a "hub of the wheeled universe," as Walt Whitman once put it. You learn experientially what has

always been true, though you have glimpsed it only rarely: that
you are the all-pervading Self, the steady space within which all
the world has sprung into existence. And that this is equally true
for everyone else. They too are the Self, they too are God, the self-
aware "inner witness" of all experience.

Because the identity of a Sadguru is not based on defensive
egotism, because he is spontaneously and wantlessly himself, we
don't need to defend ourselves when we relate to him. Whatever
else we may be afraid of, at least where he is concerned we can
safely let go, and our fearlessness, our love for him, becomes a
fulcrum, an Archemedian point enabling us to lever our mental
framework into a new shape.

Swami Muktananda is not a theologian or a philosopher in the
Western sense. Ideas concern him only as avenues to experience.
He doesn't invite us simply to think, but to become present to
ourselves in a new way. Everything about him—his voice, his
walk, his gestures, the stories he tells—is an act of instruction, a
conduit along which his energy—his *shakti*—flows, as electricity
flows along a conductive wire. His one aim is to free our locked-up
energies from the sterile labor of self defense by teaching us to
meditate. Meditation is like prayer, Baba says. It is an act of
surrender, of trust. In meditation, we gently retune our identities.
We wean ourselves from the habit of defensive egotism and create
a new habit of self-acceptance, spontaneity and fearlessness. Sitting in Baba's presence, or hearing him speak, or reading his
essays, we "catch" meditation from him and take it away with us.
For a Sadguru's job is to spread his "contagion" where it is
needed. He is a doctor who specialises in the "disease of existence," as he says, and meditation is the cure.

Like his physical presence, Baba's essays draw us toward the
experience of knowledge, not simply toward theoretical understanding. He says nothing which he has not learned experientially
for himself, and he says it so that we will learn it too. In this sense,
all of Baba's writings are in the nature of spiritual autobiography.
When he quotes from traditional Hindu texts, or from the great
mystic poets of India, it is merely to affirm in the words of other

past masters what he has revalidated in his own life. A "fully realised" master recreates the original insight of the spiritual tradition, he is a return to the beginning.

The chapters of this book contain the principal aspects of Swami Muktananda's teaching, as he expressed them in many dozens of talks throughout the United States during the two and a half years he spent here. Although I call the chapters essays, they are in fact based on transcripts of the talks themselves which I have edited so that important ideas are developed continuously in each chapter. Baba talks about the Guru, meditation, and mantra. He invokes the underlying Self which our changing emotions hide from view, and instructs us in how to reach it through meditation. There is a lyrical repetition of key images and ideas from chapter to chapter, as if Baba wanted us to remember that, for all our thinking and describing, the goal is ever the same and ever simple. One thinks of a sphere, its radius plunging always into the same center from whatever angle of approach we choose, or of the repeated developing themes of a musical composition.

The chapters of the book are liberally sprinkled with Swami Muktananda's favorite stories, for Baba believes that stories communicate the goals of the Siddha tradition more lovingly and more convincingly than mere ideas. Stories penetrate to the tender layers of our mind, they give us foreshadowings of the experience of knowledge, in its full human complexity.

Each chapter is followed by a number of questions which people have asked Baba from time to time, and the answers that he has given to clarify his teaching by connecting it to specific problems of feeling and behavior.

Message from Baba

In our search for happiness we turn our thoughts to the world outside us. Yet if we turned within and discovered the inner world, we would find everything we looked for. There is an ocean of happiness inside. In fact, whatever we look for outside can also be found inside. And inside we can revel in it.

Your happiness, which is your God, your very Self, thrives within you, and within everyone. That's why our foremost duty is to look upon others with respect and affection. That is the true religion of man. Religion is not found only in temples, mosques, synagogues and churches, but in an attitude of respect and acceptance towards others. To be pleased with others is a great attainment. That is love, and love is God.

Look for God within. The joy you seek outside is hidden within you. Uncover it. The shakti, the divine creative energy, surges within you, and is you. Experience it and you will know that there is no happiness greater than that of your own Self.

This is the message I have brought to America. People here are genuine seekers. They are sincere, straightforward, full of love and faith, and even of true renunciation. Despite the abundance of material prosperity, Americans are hungry for truth. They are looking for real unchanging happiness and will do anything to get it. America is lucky that its people, in particular the young, have taken to this path.

Seekers here have imbibed my message. They have given me lots of love. And the people who are with me have also worked very hard. As a result, I have had no difficulty in accomplishing my work here. Many Siddha Yoga meditation centers and ashrams have opened. Numerous publications, have appeared on the subject of Siddha Yoga. In two years so much work has been done. It is all a result of divine grace, of Guru's grace. For it is by the grace of my Guru that I have come here. In truth, he has done all the work, and in the future his grace will continue to flow. For the grace of a Siddha is unfailing in its effect, and those who trust it reap the benefit. They are redeemed. This process is called Siddha Yoga, the path of the Siddhas, or perfected masters. The effects of this yoga unfold spontaneously as a result of a Siddha's grace.

Truth is one and eternal. It never changes. The saints of all countries have revealed the same truth—that God is everywhere. They have become one with God. All they see is God, not individuals, sects, countries, parties and cults—not even east or west. They experience the truth in everyone and teach others to do the same. Everywhere they see equality. They have surmounted body-consciousness. They have risen beyond the man-made limitations of religious groups. Everything they do is for the benefit of all people. They are filled with compassion and remove man's suffering by their grace. They teach people to see God in each other. Such perfect beings are bestowers of grace, and their teaching is known as Siddha Yoga. My mission is to acquaint people with the power and extent of this yoga.

My teaching has no regard for cults, castes, sects, or countries. Its main point is that the truth lies within us, and that we should look for and find it there. That is why I always say: Meditate on your Self, honor your Self, worship your Self, for God dwells within you as you.

This book is not a product of the intellect alone—it does not come from reading other books, but is the outcome of direct experience. Its purpose is to help people easily understand spiritual matters. Paul Zweig's effort in bringing this book out is proof of the interest in these matters. I congratulate him for his fine work. May everyone benefit by reading it.

With love and blessings,
   Your own,
      Swami Muktananda

Entering the Inner Spaces

During my life I examined many different religions and found none that really worked; so I began to honor and worship man. I'm sure that the founders of religion meant to bring together men who had been divided through lack of love, but instead their beliefs created more separation than before. The truth is that God is not the exclusive copyright of any particular religion, for religious traditions are man-made and don't necessarily have much to do with God. I wonder if visitors to heaven or hell have seen different compartments for Hindus, Christians, Jews, and Muslims. If heaven is the same for all, then surely God is too.

A great Mahatma, Swami Ram Tirth, wrote a short story about a group of religious people who bought a piece of land to build a temple on. When the temple was finished, they consecrated it to Vishnu, hoping that many people would come to worship there. But only a few followers of Vishnu came, and that was all.

After waiting in vain for more worshipers, the trustees decided to change the deity of the temple from Vishnu to Shiva. Now the Vaishnavites stopped coming, and the temple drew a few followers of Shiva. When the Vaishnavites saw this, they stood outside and said, "Hey, where are you going? That temple was originally devoted to Vishnu."

The trustees put their heads together and decided to change the deity again. This time they installed Ganesh, but now the followers of Shiva stopped coming to the temple and stood on the road telling people, "That's not a temple of Shiva, that's a temple of Ganesh."

"All right," the trustees said, "we won't have a Hindu temple here at all; we'll build a mosque instead." So they turned the temple into a mosque. Naturally Hindus forsook the place completely; Muslims wouldn't come either because they knew it had originally belonged to Hindus.

After that the trustees built a monastery, then a prayer house, and then they tried Judaism and some Jews came. When they started praying in the Christian faith, the Jews stopped coming too. By this time the trustees were completely disgusted. "Our religions don't seem to work at all. People are so preoccupied with religious differences that one faith negates another. In fact, all these religions are a nuisance." So instead they decided to build a hotel with a nightclub on one side and a tennis court on the other. Then everybody started coming.

This is what has happened to the original ideals of love conceived by the founders of religion.

I'll tell you another story on the same subject. A peasant prayed to God, saying, "Oh, God, kindly come into my poor hut. I don't know how to worship you properly because I haven't read the Gita, the Puranas, or the Koran; I haven't read the Bible either. So I don't know the correct way to approach you. I only have love in my heart. Dearest God, I promise I'll massage your feet and make you comfortable in my bed. I'll put my own blanket over you and bathe you in warm water. I'll make bread for you from my own corn."

Meanwhile, Haszrat Musa, a religious prophet, happened to pass by and overheard this peasant's prayer. He stuck his head in the door and shouted, "Hey, come over here. What are you talking about?"

The peasant said, "I was supplicating God, asking him to please visit my hut. I said that I would feed him, offer him drink, massage his feet, and look after him in every way."

Haszrat Musa said, "You sinner. Don't you know you have

committed a gross heresy? What makes you think God has a body or a name or a shape? What makes you think that God is a man who will come to your hut, eat your rotten corn, and sleep in your stinking bed! You have insulted God, and you have insulted religion."

The peasant was frightened now and said to the prophet, "Oh, what a mistake I made. I'm sorry. I didn't mean to upset God. Please forgive me, I'll never do it again."

The peasant went his way, and the prophet returned home, where he locked himself in his room and began to pray to God in a correct manner according to rules laid down by the scriptures. In the middle of his prayers, a loud voice came down from heaven saying, "O Musa, it wasn't the peasant who committed a sin, but you. I didn't send you into this world to confuse people with differences of high and low. I sent you to bring more hearts to me. Yet this evening you turned a man away whose heart was already open to me."

Remember, no matter what method we use, we are bound to attain him with love and devotion, for God imposes no preconditions. People try to experience him in different ways, one through yoga, another through knowledge, and yet another through meditation, but God is beyond these methods. If you approach him through knowledge, you will experience him with the power of your intellect. If you approach him through meditation, you will see him with the eye of meditation. Your faith will enable you to see him in any way and anywhere. True Siddha yogis have seen him in the *sahasrar* which is the crown *chakra*, the topmost spiritual center in the head, for God has infinite power. He can do whatever he wants to do and appear to you in any form he likes.

Wherever I go, I speak of the inner truth, not of any particular religion or dogma. I speak about the innermost reality of all, which I myself have seen. I say that before you try to know what is happening around you it is of the greatest importance to know what is happening inside you. A great saint of Maharashtra, which is a part of India, wrote, "O man, you have roamed so much in the outer world. You have gone everywhere, flying from one space to another. You have picked fruit and flowers and pursued numerous activities; yet all you have earned is weariness, boredom, and constant inner smoldering. It is time now to soar in the inner spaces which are boundless. Whatever you have sought in external space, you will find in complete fullness within."

I have been in America for some time, and many people come to see me, telling the same story. They say, "I have everything, I know everything, and yet I don't feel any peace. I am suffering from anxiety. I don't know what happiness is." I receive psychiatrists who tell me that they are not at peace with themselves. I also receive their patients who tell me they have lost their peace. The doctor comes and complains, "I am not in good shape." The patients also come and say, "We are sick."

We seem to believe that another person will do something to help us; if only he or she acted in a certain way, we would be the happiest people in the world. Or, if we acted in a certain way, he or she would be the happiest person in the world. It's like the story I often tell of the tea stall and the aspirin factory. People from the tea stall go to the aspirin factory to get pills to relieve their headaches, and the people from the factory go to the tea stall for a cup of tea to relieve their headaches.

This is exactly our predicament. He looks for happiness from me and thinks that if I gave him love he would be in heaven. I look for happiness from him and think that if only he could give me love I would be in heaven. And so our days go by. In our material life we find only momentary happiness, a shadow or a reflection of true happiness.

No matter what position you hold in life, whether you are great or humble, whether you earn millions, whether you have any number of degrees and titles, enjoy the tastiest drinks, eat the most delicious foods, by the end of each day you feel tired, and all you want to do is sleep. When the time for sleep comes, you have no use for the comforts and possessions you worked so hard to get during the day. You don't even want your child or your wife around. All you want is some sleep. So you retire into a bedroom, turn off the lights, wrap a warm blanket around you, and try for a while to annihilate yourself in sleep. The next morning, if someone were to ask, "Why did you go to sleep so early last night?"

you would probably say, "I was exhausted, but now I'm feeling fresh and full of energy."

A few hours of sleep have completely refreshed you. This is the daily experience of each of us although we rarely stop to think about it or ask where the refreshment comes from that we enjoy during sleep. We haven't eaten anything, we haven't accomplished anything, yet we awaken strong and delighted. During the waking state we do so many things that we cherish; yet we wind up tired.

If you were to ask a wise man exactly what happens in sleep, he would say that your mind stops spinning around and becomes still. That's why sleep is so restful. Sages have said that the mind is the source of both our happiness and our misery; it is the cause of our bondage and of our release from bondage. In the depths of sleep, the mind gets away from its usual activities for a while, extinguishing itself in peace and stillness. As a result, it wakes up filled with vigor. The daily experience of sleep is proof that our most dependable source of energy lies within. That is why the technique of meditation was discovered.

If we could take just a little time from our busy schedules and devote it to meditation, to turning our awareness within, we would not only discover peace and contentment, but our health would also improve. We wouldn't have to take refuge in doctors so often. Man doesn't seem to care about the tremendous reserves of *shakti*, or energy, which lie dormant within him; coiled at the center of his body, *shakti* is far more powerful than electrical or even atomic energy. If we could turn our attention inward while preserving the framework of our normal lives—I never ask people to renounce their homes, their families, their jobs, just to find a little time for turning inward—these little meditations would add up. The cumulative effect would be the regeneration of our organism. We would also discover that all the instruments modern technology has given us have their spiritual counterparts within. Just as we see an entirely different world during dreams without any external aid, in meditation we would be able to see the entire cosmos without the aid of instruments.

A brilliant divine light shines within. If we could see it, our pain and misery would come to an end. The light is sweet and cooling. Its presence imparts to us what beauty we have and enables us to love one another. If it were to leave us, we would be horribly transformed.

Shakti, the divine conscious energy, resides within each of us, knowing the entire universe, perceiving it distinctly and clearly. Tolstoy told a story about a beggar who lived on a heap of gold without knowing it. He spent his entire life begging for nickels and dimes, depending on crumbs thrown to him with stingy generosity by his fellow-men. That is our condition too. Although we contain a vast unknown treasure, we spend our time in the outer world begging for whatever we can get our hands on. With these nickels and dimes of addiction, we try to become happy. It is of the utmost importance to turn our seeking inward because that is where our true wealth lies. Modern science and technology have made us the slaves of instruments. Even to understand ourselves, we seek the help of instruments. We seem to have lost faith in our capacity to see our innermost reality as it is, directly, without the intervention of external aids. The fact is, man is greater than even our wildest hopes.

In the Bhagavada Gita, Lord Krishna says, "O Arjuna, the Lord dwells within every heart." You may call it the supreme truth, you may call it love, and you may call it bliss, but it exists within your own heart. If you could devote some time after work to meditation, to diving within, you would certainly succeed in finding the treasures which lie buried there because there is nothing man cannot achieve. Do not judge yourself according to the thoughts which arise in your mind because it is the nature of the mind to think, and all kinds of thoughts, both good and bad, keep surfacing. We should turn our attention from our thoughts to their source, which is the source of the mind. That source is the Self, and it is absolutely pure, not polluted by any passing ideas. Lord Krishna says, "Though the Lord is seated within the body, within the mind, yet he is not affected at all by any of its impurities. He is not contaminated by any of its blemishes or harmful tendencies. He, the supreme truth, has taken residence within us for our sake."

Things have been so arranged that we have an easy access to that truth. If instead of wasting our time in unnecessary talk or gossip we meditated on our own inner reality, the Lord seated within would reveal himself to us without trouble.

A young couple, husband and wife, had lived happily for quite a few years on the upper floor in a building owned by a rich man. One Sunday the couple began to talk. The conversation degenerated into an argument that became increasingly violent, until their voices could be heard even a mile away. The landlord heard the screams and rushed up to see what was happening. When he saw them fighting, he was astounded and said, "You are so young, so intelligent, so well educated, why are you abusing each other this way?"

Each started to complain about the other. First, the wife said, "Look at this fool of a husband. I have been trying to convince him that our son must be a doctor because doctors make plenty of money while helping people who are in need. But my husband wants him to be a lawyer. No matter how hard I try to convince him, he won't listen to me."

The husband said, "Look at this crazy woman. I have been trying to convince her that our son has got to be a lawyer because successful lawyers get big cases to argue in court and make a fortune. He would come into contact with important people; he would have position and prestige, and everyone would seek his advice. Besides, he would only have to work during certain hours. If he were a doctor, patients would come and disturb him all the time. I don't want my boy to be harassed day and night. I want him to be a lawyer, but my wife won't listen to me."

The landlord said, "Is that all you're fighting about? It's a simple enough matter. Why don't we call the boy and ask him what he wants to do. Where is he now?"

The husband said, "The boy hasn't been born yet."

The child is yet to be born; who knows whether he will ever be born and, if he is born, what kind of person he will be. Yet the parents have started planning years ahead for him. This is what happens to our minds which are constantly engaged in planning for tomorrow and the next day and for years and years ahead. We think about distant things yet ignore what is closest to us, our own inward source.

That is why we ought to turn our awareness toward the space within, the inner self. But what does this mean? During the sleeping state all sense organs turn inward and find repose in what we call meditation. Upon turning within, the inner *shakti* is awakened, and I would like to repeat: *Shakti* is the supreme creative energy of the universe.

One may well ask, "Of what use is this inner awakening in everyday life?" First, when the *shakti* stirs, all the nerves of your body cleanse themselves spontaneously. The *shakti* eats up diseases and spreads perfect health throughout your system. A seer has written, "If your body is weak and feeble, if you cannot sleep or digest your food without pills, if you do not have enough energy in your body to function properly, what happiness can you enjoy?" Awakened *shakti* expels diseases from the system and rejuvenates it. I am a sixty-eight-year-old young man. According to the scriptures, *shakti* is the power of divine will, the eternal maiden. Once she becomes awake inside you, she injects perpetual youth into your bloodstream.

There is an extraordinary space in the heart in the form of a lotus. If your awareness could enter it, the entire cosmos would appear to you in a single place. This lovely heart-lotus is the kingdom of God. The inner *shakti kundalini* seats your mind comfortably there. What I'm describing is not a fable; I am talking from direct personal experience. Don't you see objects moving before your eyes in dreams, as though a movie were being projected on a screen? If you were to reach the enthralling space in your heart, you would be overcome by unearthly sweetness; your vision would pierce beyond the range of your sense organs.

To accomplish this inward journey, there is no need to abandon your normal pursuits because daily life in no way hinders the pursuit of God. If this vast, various world were an obstacle to God-realization, then surely God wouldn't have created it. Yet he did create it as a playground for his glory and delight.

During the first stage, the awakened *shakti* guides your awareness to the heart center. Then as you continue to meditate, she leads you upward into the *sahasrar*, the wonderful thousand-petaled lotus at the top of the head. The *shakti* rises along the central nerve until she reaches the ocular center and purifies it so that your eyes acquire the power to see even distant objects. Upon reaching the auditory center, she purifies it too, and you begin to hear God's own music. When your awareness is stabilized in the spiritual center between the eyes, the center of divine fragrance, such subtle smells are released that you are overwhelmed. No external perfumes could surpass this fragrance. When God created this beautiful sinless body, he planted his own light inside it; therefore it is wrong to think of the body as corrupt or depraved or as something made of dust. The Gita says one is one's own best friend and one's own worst enemy. Our own thoughts and desires are responsible for the ugliness around us or the heaven around us.

As you go deeper into your Self through meditation, you will see a brilliant light whose effulgence is a million times brighter than sunlight. Again, this is no theory but an actual experience. At the center of the effulgence the Blue Pearl sparkles and scintillates all the time. That pearl is our very life, the center of our consciousness and our existence, and it is very dynamic. Though it dwells in the body, it doesn't touch any constituents of the body. When a meditator's gaze turns upward, he or she sees this Blue Pearl sparkling and shining. The Blue Pearl is man's inner reality. You see it come out of one eye, stand in front of you, go back to its place inside, and then come out through the other eye at the speed of lightning. The Blue Pearl shimmers and vibrates all the time, and its vibrations produce melodious music which fills the meditator with rapture until he begins to dance. That pearl is called the inner Self, the inner *atman*, or the inner *shakti* in the scriptures. It has such power that it can travel to any world no matter how distant and return in a moment. Call it the light of God if you like. It is full of boundless peace, bliss, and ecstasy, and we can know it only through our direct experience.

Though such divinity dwells within us, we hurry from door to door, begging and groveling. We could experience inner awakening and see the Blue Pearl by a mere touch of a Sadguru.

I would like to tell you another story. A man went from place to place seeking happiness and fulfillment. Finally he sat down under a tree which we call Kalpataru the wish-fulfilling tree, because it grants whatever wish arises in your mind. He found the shade of the tree cool and soothing, and he thought, "This is such a beautiful tree. If only I had a small house here." The moment the wish took form in his mind a beautiful house appeared in front of him. Then he thought, "If I could find a lovely woman, my happiness would be complete," and a nymphlike woman appeared. "If only I had some good things to eat, my delight would know no end," and the food appeared too. He wished for a butler to serve him; a butler appeared to serve the sumptuous food, and the man enjoyed it all immensely. After his stomach was full, he began to think again, "I wonder what's happening here? Whatever I wish for seems to appear. I wished for a house, a girl, food, a butler, and they all came. Could there be a goblin living in this tree?" The goblin loomed before him. "I wonder if he's going to eat me up?" And the goblin ate him up. This is what we do to ourselves. Although the most amazing Blue Pearl, the highest divinity, dwells right at the top of our head, we consider ourselves to be insecure, unhappy creatures.

Another great saint of our country, Jnaneshwar, says, "If you want to see a magnificent and beautiful sight, then roam in the inner spaces. . . . The Blue Pearl vibrates there, and melodious harmonies arise. When this divine music begins to thunder, a drop of elixir falls from the inner sky, touches the root of the tongue, and you soar as high as you can possibly get. Nothing in the outer world, no juice, no drink, compares with this elixir. When it reaches the heart, it spreads to all seventy-two thousand nerves of the body, and you become young from within, though from outside you may still look old." Therefore, gaze within. If you could internalize your awareness, you would be able to see an amazing blue light spreading through all the nerves of your body.

Q: Can I gain something from a Guru without giving up my religion?

Baba: Why not? What religion does sleep belong to? If he wishes, a Hindu may call it Hindu sleep; a Christian, Christian sleep; a Muslim, Muslim sleep. The truth is that meditation is everybody's own personal religion. The inner Self doesn't distinguish among Hinduism, Christianity, and Islam. A Brahmin priest may say that God is high above, but if he experiences any joy in singing God's name, it will be in his own heart. A Muslim *maulvi* may raise his hands toward the sky and call, "Allah, Allah," but if he receives even a little grace from God, he will experience it within.

Q: Must I consider my work as a businessman an obstacle on the spiritual path?

Baba: Toward the end of the Gita, Lord Krishna answers this question when he says, "The same supreme being stretches in all directions. All activities and pursuits, all names and forms in this world, are only different manifestations of the truth." Anyone who worships God following his vocation is fulfilling the purpose of his birth. For example, a musician can worship God with music, provided he has no selfish motive. A teacher can worship God by teaching what he has to teach, provided he teaches selflessly. A businessman can worship God, providing he does it without selfish desire. A peasant can worship God by raising crops in his fields, provided he does it selflessly. By doing it selflessly I mean dedicating it to God. No matter what your pursuit in the world, if you dedicate it to God, it becomes a spiritual pursuit. No matter what your field of activity, if you were to follow it without personal desire for its fruits, that too would be great yoga.

Q: I wonder if the *shakti* can make one a better bricklayer, a better doctor, or a better baker?

Baba: Your question is beautiful. If the *shakti* or inner awakening did not enable you to function better in your outer life, what would be the point of it? The *shakti* that I speak of is not some ordinary energy. It is *chiti*, the energy of consciousness, which creates and permeates the entire cosmos. It is the very *shakti* which lies dormant within us and becomes active through *shaktipat*. Once that happens, it is perfectly capable of taking care of our outer life too. In fact, it improves our outer life to an immeasurable degree. A doctor's intuition will become more subtle so that he can diagnose diseases with fewer instruments; a bricklayer will become expert in his craft; a warrior will fight with greater vigor; a baker will bake the rays of *shakti* into his bread and make it more delectable. The *shakti* affects not only humans but also animals, plants, and trees. If you have time, come to our ashram in India and see what giant mangoes grow on our trees. We grow so many different kinds of fruits and vegetables. *Shakti* also affects animals very deeply. When I used to visit the cows in our cowshed, sometimes the milk would start to come spontaneously and pour onto the floor. *Shakti* is the energy of exuberance and joy, stirring the heart of every creature.

Q: While spiritual seeking helps the individual lead a positive life, the impact on society as a whole is meager. Is there a way to help larger numbers of people who have not yet been persuaded to lead a more positive life?

Baba: Only one who eats food feels satisfaction; only one who sleeps receives the joy of restfulness; only one who bathes is touched by cool water. Likewise, only one who practices *sadhana* will find life becoming more positive and beautiful. If you were to spread meditation in society, then others would have the same experience. Meditation is a means for attaining the inner center of rest, and this is open to every human being, not just to one. If other people were to practice *sadhana* and meditation, they too would become peaceful and happy, and the atmosphere of all society would change.

God exists not only within but also without. Therefore, the first step is to achieve awareness of the all-pervasive being who exists in the outside world. There will always be conflicts because this world is made of the three *gunas*, and no matter what system of government is in power in a country, the enforcement of law will involve a certain amount of repression. If you want to do something in the political field, you are most welcome to, but remember, the people who oppose you are human beings just as you are. One who is your friend today may become your enemy tomorrow, and one who is your enemy today may become your friend the day after. It is good to work toward improving the world through political action, provided that you look upon the people involved with the right attitude, which is to honor them and to love the Self in them.

Q: Does Baba dream in a different way since his realization?

Baba: I dream only rarely, but when I do, my dreams are usually prophetic. Sometimes I see people on their way to meet me, or I see the actual meeting taking place. But since I don't sleep much, I have few dreams. Normally I fall asleep in a meditative state which continues until I wake up. That's what you should do too. Glide into sleep while repeating your mantra, and the mantra will continue throughout your sleep.

The bliss of the *turiya*, or transcendental state, is great. Just one hour of *turiya* is equal to one thousand hours of deep sleep. That's why I need so little sleep. If I go to bed at midnight, I'm up at three o'clock. Just as, in your present condition, you experience dreams in sleep, if you were to meditate long enough, you would experience meditation in your sleep. The bliss of the Self is greater than the bliss of sleep. If there were no joy in it, why would we meditate at all?

Q: Would you comment on the liberation of women in America? Is that the hope of the future, for men as well as women?

Baba: Liberation is everyone's birthright, regardless of sex. Only in our ordinary life does the distinction between man and woman have some meaning. For God, it has no meaning. God only knows the inner Self which is neither man nor woman. To begin with, merely to come into existence, every man, whether he's a priest or a president, needs a woman. If you were to understand your physical nature, you would become aware that every body is part male and part female. So if you are a man, you already contain woman; if you are a woman, you already contain man. In a man, the masculine elements predominate; in a woman, the feminine elements. That's the only difference. The first and most important Guru for every child, male or female, is its mother. Some people may think that women are inferior, but Indian scriptures do not approve of that view. For example, we find nothing wrong with women being priests.

You Are Who You Think You Are

In an important passage of the Bhagavad Gita, Krishna declares, "O Arjuna, this body is said to be a field." The Sanskrit word for field is *kshetra*, meaning a plot of farm land. Such land is innocent and pure, for it takes on whatever character the farmer chooses to give it, multiplied many times. A few grains of wheat become a crop. A handful of corn is turned into a harvest. Land will not resist your intention, for the law of the field seems to be that it will increase whatever you have put into it. You can choose to create a garden that will delight the hearts of all who visit it, or a guest house to provide hospitality for your friends, or a temple where people can come and perform worship.

On the other hand, you can turn land into a cemetery, or you can use it as a dumping ground for people to come and unload all their garbage. The Lord calls this body a field because you can accomplish in it what you choose. In this very body you can become a sensualist and entrap yourself in purely mundane activities, or you can withdraw from the mechanical routine of everyday life and concentrate on the inner spaces. What you sow here and now, you will harvest later. Therefore, you must sow God in this body by meditating on him. Devisingh, a great poet-saint of India, has written: "O man, you are most fortunate to have been born into a human form because within it dwells the Lord himself. You can be sure that you will not be born in this form many times again. Therefore, strive to realize the Lord within."

I once read a story about a painter who wanted to create the image of an ideal young man. He searched throughout the kingdom until, finally, he found exactly the model he was looking for. The young man he had found was lovely and noble in every way, and the portrait turned out quite well. The painter was rewarded handsomely by the government, and many copies were made and put up at different points in the city.

After some time, the painter decided to create the portrait of a man who was the complete opposite of the one he had painted earlier. He began to look for a model who had all the worst qualities—who would pick pockets, commit thefts, use drugs, and murder people without compunction. He went from town to town, city to city, and street to street looking for a model; yet he couldn't find anyone who matched the image he had in his mind. At last he decided to go to the general prison and look for a suitable subject there. This prison was terribly crowded. Thousands of prisoners were inside, and he scrutinized each one carefully. After he had seen a thousand or two, he finally came upon the perfect character. The man was absolutely brutal, merciless, his body was in ruins, and the marks of degradation were visible in every part of him. He was quite young, hardly twenty years old; yet he had already lived a terrible and varied life.

The artist painted the young man's portrait and then showed the portrait to the government authorities, explaining that it was the antithesis of his earlier painting of the perfect hero. The art academy rewarded him for this one too which was called the portrait of the worst man on earth. The authorities ordered copies of both portraits to be hung side by side at important points in the town so that people could see both and become keenly aware of the contrast between good and evil.

Inside the prison, too, many copies of the portraits were put up. When the prisoner who had been the painter's model saw them side by side, he began to beat his head and lament and cry, "Alas, alas."

People were amazed. They came to him and said, "We have never seen you weep before. Why are you weeping?"

"How can I explain what has happened? Both these portraits

are of me. Once I was beautiful and noble as in this first picture. Then my life went wrong, and I fell and kept on falling until I became as you see me in the second portrait."

Therefore, Lord Krishna says, "Arjuna, this body is like a field; care for it well." Within it lives the farmer, the owner of the field. His name is the supreme Lord, or the highest truth.

One day Lord Buddha sat under a tree on the bank of a river during a phase of his life when he was practicing severe austerities. After a while a group of seekers from a neighboring village passed his way singing a song for their own delight which said, "O singer, don't draw the strings of your lute too tightly lest they break, but don't leave them slack either, for they would not make music." These words penetrated the Buddha's heart. He saw that his body, which was made of food, was like a stringed instrument. By mortifying it he was defeating his own purpose, while if he indulged it, it would become soft and flabby and waste away. Instead, he understood that he should keep to the middle path.

Meditation, seeking within, is the middle path. It avoids the extremes of too much or too little tightening. In India, seers have called it Sahaj Yoga (natural yoga). Other names have been Siddha Yoga (perfect yoga) and Maha Yoga (great yoga). Its glory lies in that it can be practiced easily while living your normal life, meeting your worldly responsibilities. For this, however, you need the Guru's grace. Another seer has said, "Few can know the trick of merging into the inner reality spontaneously and naturally, without the grace of a Siddha Guru, or a perfected master."

What do we mean by a Siddha? A Siddha lives in total freedom. He is not subject to the pull of the outgoing senses or to the cravings and desires which arise in the mind. He lives in a place beyond the body. There are many sorts of Gurus and teachers, and I wish all of them well because all may contribute to our growth at different stages. Nonetheless, many people these days ask, "What is the point of having a Guru?" When this question is put to me, I say, "Listen, when you feel sick, you go to a doctor; when you want to build a house, you go to an architect; when you need a haircut, you go to a hairdresser; and when you want to have your clothes washed, you go to a launderer. Why should you have any

objection to the poor Guru? You turn to all these different special-
ists to answer particular needs. I can assure you that the Guru also
answers a certain need which is very deep."

According to Shaivite philosophy, the philosophy of the Siddhas, or perfected beings, a Guru is the divine power of grace; in
other words, a Guru can transmit divine grace into a disciple,
thereby awakening the disciple's inner *shakti* and piercing his
chakras, or inner centers. To his spouse, Parvati, Lord Shiva says,
"O goddess, there is no shortage of Gurus who steal their students'
wealth, but one is rare who would steal the restlessness of a student's mind." A Siddha Guru is able to transmit *shakti* to a disciple simply by means of a glance. As long as we have not met
such a master on our journey, we are bound to have a difficult
time.

One morning St. Augustine strolled along the seashore. The sun
was rising on the horizon. He had been seeking God day and
night, and his eyes were tired and heavy. His head too was bowed
down as if he were carrying a great weight on it, and in fact he
was. He was weighed down by the different scriptures he had read,
by the logical systems he had studied, by the words he had spoken
for so many years, and by the different disciplines he had followed
one after another.

That morning as he walked, he encountered a boy anxiously
holding a cup in his hand. St. Augustine was intrigued and said,
"My son, what is wrong? Why do you seem so worried this morning? And why are you holding that cup in your hand?"

The boy answered, "Sir, you seem no less anxious and bur-
dened. Maybe you could tell me what is weighing on your heart.
What has produced such heaviness in you? And where is your
cup?"

St. Augustine was amused and said, "What cup are you talking
about? All that matters to me is seeking God. I long to know
him."

The boy said, "Sir, I am trying to find a way to hold the ocean
in this cup, but I'm not having any luck. That's why I'm anxious
and worried. All I think about is how to achieve my goal."

When Augustine heard these words, his eyes were opened, and

understanding dawned in his heart. He realized that he had been trying to hold the ocean of the infinite in the tiny cup of his ego and that he could never succeed. Unless he threw the cup into the sea, he would never achieve what he longed for. Only if he threw the cup into the sea, would the sea fill it inside and out. Thus he became aware of the cup of his intellect, the cup of his ego, and of the infinite ocean of the love of God surging in his heart. He had only to merge that cup into the ocean, and he would attain his goal. Augustine flung the cup into the sea, and the cup became the sea.

That boy is not a lone case. Thousands of boys hold their own little cups and stand on the seashore. They argue with one another about whose cup is bigger, who will be able to hold more of the ocean in his cup, whose is better, and whose worse. Because the ocean will not come into their cups, they stand anxiously on the shore.

There is only one bondage, and that is the bondage of ego. Everything God has created is beautiful, except perhaps the ego, for ego is at the root of our deterioration and of all harm and evil.

A great saint in India, Eknath Maharaj, had studied all the scriptures thoroughly and had composed great philosophical works. When his life's task was finished, he said, "Now I am going to give you the secret of God-realization in one phrase: 'If you can dissolve your ego, you will reach the goal.' "

Ego has kept us separate from God and has made us small, insecure. It is responsible for our jealousy and greed, and it keeps us smoldering all the time. No matter how much learning you have, no matter how many miracles you can perform, ego will never let up on you. Our power cannot exceed the power of ego; so often we seem to be small toys for the ego to play with.

I would like to tell you another story. A ferry on the bank of a river was loaded down with everything the ferryman could possibly put into it. When he was finished, he tried to push off, but the ferry wouldn't move. He thought maybe he had loaded it too heavily; so he took some items out and pushed it again, but it still wouldn't budge. He began to wonder if the ferry was under the curse of an evil spirit; so he broke a coconut, considered auspicious in our country, and he cut a lemon, also considered auspicious, but that didn't work. Then he called a priest, and the priest made him perform a ritual which didn't have the slightest effect. He began to repeat a mantra and even that did not help him. Looking around he saw a holy man, a *sadhu*, bathing in the river near the other bank, and he shouted, "O Babaji, O Babaji, will you help me? My boat doesn't move."

"You fool," the *sadhu* called, "do you know that your boat is tied to the dock by a rope? Unless you untie the rope how can the boat move?"

Many of us are as foolish as that man. We want the ferry of our seeking to move out, but we don't untie the rope of ego which keeps it firmly attached to our limited existence. Therefore, instead of repeating, "I am, I am, I am," all the time, why don't you repeat, "*So'ham, So'ham, So'ham,*" which means, "I am that," in other words, "I am God, I am he."

God is closer to us than anything in the world. He is our innermost reality. But to find your Self within, to have your *shakti* awakened, you need yogis, Gurus, or *sadhus;* you need holy men, because a Guru can help you get into meditation spontaneously. As you plunge within, you discover a most wonderful space in the heart; from there, moving upward toward the divine center in the head, you become absorbed in joy, ecstasy, bliss. You are freed from boredom and anxiety. In the Gita, Krishna says to Arjuna: "The world outside is constantly changing, nothing lasts. If you live continually with external things, your life will be sorrowful. Therefore you must discover the space within and begin to live there, for the bliss and beauty of the inner realms are unceasing. One who lives there does not know misery or sorrow." Otherwise man rushes around madly day and night. He is looking for peace and finds only peacelessness. He wants fulfillment, but he finds only despair.

There was a man who was scared of his own shadow and also didn't like his footprints. All his life he tried to get away from them, but no matter how madly he rushed around, his shadow and his footprints always chased after him. One day he thought,

"Maybe I could get rid of these monsters if I marched left right, left right." But the more he marched, the more the shadow and footprints marched after him. He began to march more quickly, and the monsters pursued him at the same speed. After a while he began to run, and they also began to run. When he looked back, he said, "They are still chasing after me. I'd better run faster," and he ran faster and still faster. Then he began to gallop, and the shadow and footprints galloped after him. At last he collapsed, the shadow closed in, and he died.

The saint who told this story remarks, "This man was a fool. If, instead of running away madly from his shadow and footprints, he had found a huge tree and reposed in the shade of that tree, the shadow would have disappeared and so would the footprints." If, instead of running around feverishly all the time, we entered the inner space and sat under the vast and beautiful tree of peace, we would overcome our anxiety and find what we have always looked for; stillness and fulfillment. A most amazing peace thrives within. Whatever small satisfaction we get from eating, drinking, and other forms of pleasure is only an outward ripple of this deep inner peace, a mere reflection of what exists inside us. That is why it's important to take a genuine interest in meditation.

We ought to learn a lesson from our everyday experience. We eat, yet it doesn't bring us lasting peace; we drink, and that doesn't help either. We are compelled to eat and drink again. We meet friends, earn money, and still have no durable contentment. Yet if we meditated, we would find it easily. If we enjoyed the grace of the inner being, we would surmount suffering even while living in the world. The blue light pervades everyone of us. Inward seeking, meditation on the Self, is the highest worship and the best of all prayers to God.

King Bhartruhari was a very great yogi. In the heyday of his youth he passed his scepter to his son so he could retire to a cave in the forest solitudes and begin to meditate on the Self. He composed a number of works, among which is the following story about a bee.

Once a bee was drunk on his youth. He flitted from flower to flower, sipping their nectar, and his days and nights passed in a state of blind intoxication. One day this bee flew until he reached a lake in which stood a beautiful lotus. The bee settled on the lotus and began to drink so deeply that he lost his sense of time. He wasn't even aware the sun had set and darkness had fallen. The lotus closed, and even then the bee could have escaped by biting his way through, but he didn't care, thinking, "The night will pass quickly. Day will come, and when the rays of the sun touch the lotus, its petals will open again, and I will fly away and bring my wife and family and all my relations so they too can feast on the flower. And they will all thank me for such a great pleasure."

Soon it was midnight. A big brother of the bee, an elephant who was equally drunk, left his home in the forest and began to roam through the night pulling down trees until finally he arrived at the pond. The elephant was thirsty and began to drink. Then he was hungry; so he picked one lotus and then another until he came to the one encompassing the bee. He picked that too and chewed it while the bee made a worried sound. All the beautiful dreams about his friends and family were cut off right there, and the bee cried out, "Alas, I didn't escape when I could, and now I have been crushed between the teeth of an elephant."

There is no point in feeling superior to this bee because each of us is a bee pursued by a mad elephant, death. That is why Bhartruhari says, "Man, as long as your body is healthy and strong, as long as your senses are keen and your mind functions, as long as old age is far away and you have many years to live, meditate on the inner Self. Move in the inner space and find what you must find inside."

Start meditating with a quiet mind right now this very moment. Foolish people think, "We can start meditating when old age comes and we have nothing else to do. There is plenty of time for that crazy business." But Bhartruhari says, "Don't forget, you are behaving like a man who rushes around to dig a well because his house has caught fire." God has endowed man with tremendous capacities. The supreme truth lives right within him; therefore he should dive ever more deeply within himself.

I have talked about my experience of the Blue Pearl. It is as tiny as a sesame seed, and it is the most beautiful, fascinating sight you could ever see. It is also supremely intelligent and will guide you from within if you turn to it. The Blue Pearl has the power to assume new forms. It can appear in meditation and bring a message you may badly need at that moment. You can see the entire cosmos inside the Blue Pearl. This is no fable but a fact. The innermost reality lives within you, and you can see it in meditation. Therefore, I always say, "Meditate on your Self, honor and worship your Self, kneel to your Self because the supreme truth lives within you as you."

A poet-saint of Maharashtra has written a song in which he says: "In order to worship, you first create a temple and then install an idol in it, imagining God to be present within the idol. Then you worship the idol, recite hymns to it, and bring it fruit. Not the smallest deed or act you perform goes to waste because your acts launch vibrations into the atmosphere which are reflected back to you. By worshiping the image intensely, you realize God within it; yet God actually dwells within you. If you were to worship your Self, would it surprise you to find God where he is, inside yourself?"

Q: In order to wipe out one's ego, can one overcome the tendency to seek praise by an attitude of self-deploration or self-condemnation?

Baba: Self-praise doesn't do much good, and those who are given to it fall into all sorts of traps. For example, they practice, or pretend to practice, certain disciplines for the sake of praise alone. But whenever you depend on others for anything, whether it is praise or something else, you become a beggar. Instead of desiring praise from others, one should be satisfied with one's own Self. One who becomes a disciple in order to receive praise will be severely tested by his Guru. I have had disciples tell me again and again that they had seen the Blue Pearl and had seen me within the Blue Pearl and had surrendered fully to me. I said to them, "You had better be careful about what you are saying because anyone who has seen the Blue Pearl has also achieved complete humility and would never make any claims about it."

A person addicted to music will hum or sing even when nobody is there to hear him. He sings because he is in love with singing and has become its victim.

Both praise and self-condemnation are beside the point. What matters is faith in the Self, devotion to the Self. It is absurd to court praise from people about your great devotion and surrender. Your actions alone matter. Otherwise, when the Guru pretends to flare up even slightly at a student, the student takes his loincloth and runs away.

A Marathi poem narrates the story of a generous person who gave milk to a beggar every day for twelve years. One day the beggar asked for some buttermilk, but there wasn't any in the house that day, and the rich man told him so. The beggar immediately flared up and began to shout at his benefactor, "What a miser you are! You have so much wealth; you have herds of cows. A river of milk flows in your house; yet I come for a little buttermilk, and you say no!"

That beggar received milk for twelve years; yet one little refusal made him hot with anger. In the same way a disciple turns away from his Guru and complains because he is not given honor or praise on a certain occasion. But what difference can praise make to inner attainment? Is such a disciple worthy of being a disciple? The truth is that he is not interested in spiritual progress or the Guru-disciple relationship at all. He is only interested in business. Until now he had earned a lot through a worldly trade, and now after seeing that spiritual goods have started to sell on the market, he turns to the spirit and begins to sell spiritual goods. He is not interested in inner enlightenment but only in self-glory.

Self-praise and self-condemnation are equally useless. What counts is your actions and your faith in the inner Self.

Q: What is the soul?

Baba: According to Vedanta, there is nothing to which the soul can be compared. The soul is simply the soul. However, a few analogies may be helpful. The soul is that which activates the inner psychic organs and the outer sense organs. The soul is the witness, the watcher, the seer of all the activities of waking, dreaming, and deep sleep. The soul exists at the junction between the incoming and outgoing breaths.

This is one way of understanding what the soul is, but if you want to experience the nature of the soul, you have to close your eyes and become completely silent. Only in inner stillness can the soul be experienced.

Q: Isn't it hard to work after the mind has been dissolved?

Baba: Don't take that expression literally. I don't mean that the mind ceases to function or that one loses consciousness. Just as water acquires the color of anything it comes in contact with, so does the mind. When the color of water changes, the water does not cease to be water. Similarly, when the mind merges into the inner Self, it doesn't cease to function, it is not destroyed. Some people have an irrational fear in this matter because they don't understand what the phrase "dissolution of the mind" means.

What is the nature of the mind? It is not an inert substance but the element of consciousness itself. When that energy is directed outward, it becomes what we call the mind. When it turns into itself, then we say that the mind has been dissolved. Our sages have defined the Self of the world, the inner Self, as that which, though it lives in the mind, is yet separate from the mind. It cannot be known by the mind because the mind is its body. It makes the mind active; it is inner consciousness, the purest nectar. As long as that inner consciousness functions, a therapist need not fear that the mind will cease to function.

Q: What is *karma?* Can we ever be free from it?

Baba: Karma results from the activities of the outer and the inner sense organs, particularly those activities which are motivated by desire. There are three kinds of *karma: prarabdha, sanchit,* and *kriyaman. Sanchit* is the *karma* which has accumulated during our previous incarnations. *Prarabdha* is the portion of *sanchit* which is presently active. *Kriyaman* results from our current actions and will bear fruit at some future time. *Karma* binds the soul. Past *karma* compels the soul to earn more *karma* and to suffer its consequences whether we like it or not, for it acts through us by force. The seers have said that *karma* cannot be exhausted until it has been worked out.

Here is a story which illustrates what I am saying. It was raining, and the river was in flood. A bear had been swept away by the rapid flow of water. He had no hope of living nor could he die, floundering desperately with his four limbs. Two friends were sitting on the bank, and one said, "Look, there is a beautiful black robe floating down the river." Without stopping to think, the other jumped into the river and tried to grab hold of the robe with both hands, but the bear grabbed him with all four paws. Both struggled to keep from drowning. The bear tried to push the man down by getting on top of him, and the man tried to push the bear down by getting on top of him. Together they were swept down the river. The man began to cry to his friend for help, and the friend shouted, "Let go of the robe and come back to shore."

"I'm letting go of the robe," the drowning friend cried, "but the robe won't let go of me."

Karma is like that bear: Once it has grabbed you, it won't let go. You can be free of *karma* only when you attain the state of *akarma*, or actionlessness. Lord Krishna says to Arjuna, "Through meditation kindle the fire of knowledge within you, and that fire will burn away all your *karma*; it will consume your impurities and your sins, rendering you innocent and pure."

Q: I would like to know how to handle an overwhelming sense of loneliness.

Baba: Once the Prophet Mohammed was going on a pilgrimage with two of his friends. On the way some bandits started chasing them. Mohammed's friends became very agitated, and the prophet asked them, "Are you afraid?"

"Yes," they said, "some bandits are chasing after us."

The prophet said, "Are you aware of the being who stands behind us and who is equal to any number of bandits?"

Because you have given him up, you feel lonely. Grab hold of him now, and then there will be two of you, God and yourself. The sense of loneliness will vanish. When such a powerful Lord pervades everywhere, why should one feel lonely?

Q: Sometimes I receive an impulse from within, like an inner voice, which urges me to do this or that. Should I consider this to be the voice of the Self and do what it says?

Baba: It is the mind's nature to be friendly sometimes, and other times antagonistic; sometimes pleased, at other times displeased. Sixteen kinds of feeling pass constantly through the mind. Therefore you should not attach much importance to the inner voice; as long as your mind is subject to these changes, its impulses will not always be true. Only after you have achieved perfect realization will your inner voice become completely dependable. Until one has seen the blue light in his *sahasrar* and his deity within that light, the inner voice must not be relied upon, for it is still tainted with the different *gunas*, sometimes with *tamo*, sometimes with *rajo*, and sometimes with *sattva guna*. So you should not attach much importance to it. During the period of *sadhana* you should listen to the one who has initiated your *sadhana* and not depend much on your inner inspiration. However, once your *sadhana* is consummated, you can rely totally on the inner inspiration. The Lord says in the Gita that whatever thoughts arise in the mind, whether favorable or unfavorable, are products of the interplay of the three *gunas*. The Lord tells Arjuna to transcend the three *gunas* and become free from them.

Q: If India is the homeland of creative knowledge, why is there so much misery there? Why isn't it a paradise?

Baba: The Vedantic paradise is not a physical place which you can locate in the outside world. When a heart fills with Vedantic knowledge, it becomes its own paradise. If you have eyes to see, you will see it where it is: pervading the inner place, not outside.

I would like to tell you a story about the importance of faith. In Delhi the Moghul King Akbar used to recite the Koran every day under the guidance of his priest. One day he asked the priest, "What is the proper way to receive the instructions of the Koran? How much faith can we have in its truth?"

The priest answered, "I'll answer your question tomorrow or the day after."

That evening the recitation of the Koran was held as usual. But the next day when it was time for the recitation to begin, the priest came in and started to shout, "Your majesty, the bridge across the Jamuna River has been stolen. You had better send your soldiers to retrieve it right away." Immediately Akbar sounded the horn, and his soldiers came running. He ordered them to hurry to the Jamuna and catch whoever was running away with the bridge. The soldiers marched in full strength, but when they reached the spot, they found the bridge still there.

"Your majesty," they said upon returning to the palace, "the bridge is where it was. The person who gave you the news doesn't know what he's talking about."

Then the priest, who was reciting the Koran, stopped and said, "Your majesty, you should receive the Koran as confidently as you received news about the bridge being stolen. You know as well as I do that a bridge isn't a small object that someone can carry away in his pocket. But since your priest said it had been stolen, you accepted his word with full faith. That is the sort of faith you should have in the Koran."

The Guru

The Guru is a commodity that sells at a fantastic price on the American market. One Guru prescribes tantric techniques, another gives you a mantra, a third gives philosophical discourses. Gurus teach the yoga of alcohol, the yoga of promiscuity, and the yoga of drugs. Gurus are getting richer and richer, and their students, poorer and poorer. Some Indian Gurus, after coming here, have become four-armed gods. Because Americans are rather credulous and naive in this matter, any Guru proves to be a smash hit. But everything will be all right because Americans have beautiful hearts and a willingness to accept the teachings of a true master. India has exported quite a large number of Gurus to your country because it's hard to survive as a Guru in India. Here, it doesn't seem to be any trouble at all.

I read the story of Laila and Majanu in a book by Swami Ram Tirth. They are the Indian Romeo and Juliet, and their story has become a legend. Majanu was the son of a washerman, and Laila was a princess, the daughter of the king of the land. One day Majanu's father asked him to take the royal laundry to the palace. While there, he happened to catch a glimpse of Laila, and as destiny would have it, he became intoxicated with love for her. Majanu almost went crazy. He felt rooted to the spot, and the palace guards had a hard time throwing him out.

After that, Majanu became completely immersed in Laila and started repeating the mantra, "Alas, Laila, alas my darling, alas, my beloved." Instead of repeating, "Rama, Rama," all he could say was, "Laila, Laila, Laila." Majanu was so absorbed in Laila that he completely forgot about himself. Other people had to give him food and clothing, for he had become absolutely incapable of looking after his needs.

When Laila heard of Majanu's love for her, she was deeply moved. From her room on the top floor of the palace she would see him walking the streets crying, "Laila, Laila, Laila." After awhile, she caught the infection too and started crying, "Majanu, Majanu, Majanu."

Now they were even; Majanu meditated on Laila, and Laila meditated on Majanu, and they lost sight of everything else in the world. Though their love had started with ordinary passion, gradually it became more refined, more absorbing, until finally it was completely purged of passion. Majanu was so possessed by the purity of his love that he transcended the sexual appetite and the sense organs, attaining a state in which Laila might actually have stood in front of him and he would not have recognized her. The same happened with Laila. Even if Majanu had held her and touched her, she would not have responded because she was absorbed, as was he, in the purity of inner love. Pushpadantacharya, a great sage, composed a marvelous hymn to Shiva in which he wrote, "It's a pity that people do not know the bliss of the Self, compared to which the muck of sensual enjoyment is wholly tasteless."

Majanu and Laila transcended the sensual pull and became absorbed in each other's purest form. As Majanu lost awareness of his body, his outer condition became pitiful. He couldn't eat or drink, he went about in rags, his head was bare to the sun. People reported his condition to the king, saying, "Your majesty, Majanu has fallen into a most pitiful state; you ought to do something for him."

The king's heart was touched. He issued a royal command that all shopkeepers should provide Majanu with whatever he needed and send the bills to the royal treasury.

Businessmen will be businessmen. Their only care is to make money even at the expense of the king. So the shopkeepers pro-

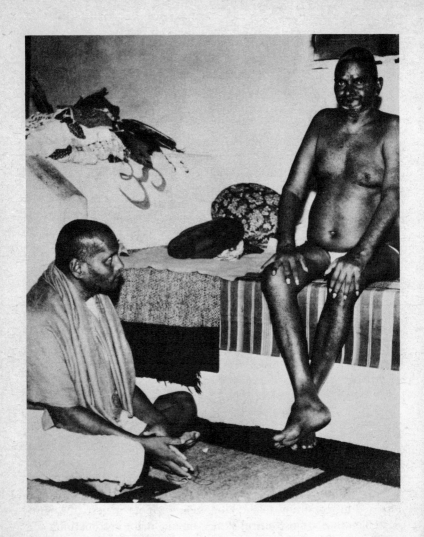

vided abundantly for Majanu: Cloth merchants gave him dozens of new shirts, bakers brought him more bread than he could eat, shoe merchants fitted him with a new pair of shoes each day, and all the bills were sent to the royal treasury.

Meanwhile, there were plenty of young men around town who,

when they saw Majanu, began to think, "That's a good life." Bored with their jobs and their studies, they thought, "If I were Majanu, I'd get everything free." So they decided to become Majanus, and their number began to swell to the delight of the shopkeepers who sent all the bills to the king. If someone didn't like his boss, he quit his job and became a Majanu. If someone didn't like school, he left and became a Majanu. If a boy thought his parents were treating him too strictly, he left home and became a Majanu. By the end of the month, the expenditures on Majanu had risen to a million dollars. The treasurer complained to the king, "Your majesty, I'm afraid the number of Majanus has increased so much that we can't afford to pay the bills anymore."

The king was unnerved. He had offered to provide for one Majanu, and now there were a thousand. So he asked his prime minister for advice. The prime minister said, "Your majesty, you yourself are responsible. You issued an order that Majanu should be clothed and fed free of charge, and now all the good-for-nothings in town have become Majanus. But don't worry, your majesty, I'll take care of it."

The prime minister called a press conference and instructed the reporters to put this news item in their papers: On the fifteenth day of the month, all Majanus will be hanged.

The moment the Majanus heard this news, they panicked. One threw away his hat; another threw away his pants; a third threw away his shirt; a fourth threw away his shoes. One ran to Mexico, another to France, a third to Pakistan, a fourth to Europe. On the morning of the fifteenth day of the month, only one Majanu was left in the streets, crying, "Laila, Laila, Laila." He wasn't at all conscious of what had happened or of the king's order. He was the real Majanu. A messenger came to him and said, "Majanu, the king wants to come and meet you. When would be a good time?"

And Majanu answered, "He can come whenever he likes, but he must come as Laila, for Laila is all I see."

This is what has happened today. Plenty of yogi Majanus appear because it is quite profitable to be a yogi. You are honored and respected; you can charge a fee and pass off any technique you like to credulous people. If the government were to pass a law against yogis operating in this country, they would all disappear before you could turn around. Only the real one would remain, the one to whom the hanging noose doesn't mean a thing.

Therefore, if you are on the spiritual path, you should keep your eyes open and watch where you are going. When you meet a Guru, first see how much of his own teaching he has imbibed. If he is teaching knowledge, you must try to find some evidence of the effect of knowledge in his own person. If he is teaching devotion, you must find some evidence, however faint, of devotion. The other day a yogi who is quite respected and has a large following came to see me. He had a pot belly, and he said that he had been teaching yoga. I asked him whether he himself practiced yoga, and he said, "I gave that up long ago; now I only teach it."

People teach meditation, but they themselves don't meditate. People teach yoga which they themselves don't practice. A true Guru would not make things so cheap. He would test people first and then initiate them. Likewise, students should test a Guru before accepting him. Anyone who claims to be a Guru must be totally disciplined; he must exercise self-control in food and drink, in talk, and in everything else. A yogi's only addiction is yoga. Though he may meet people and spend time with them, his vision is always focused on his inner Self. Though he may hear what people say, only the inner music penetrates his eardrums. Though his body may move around, inside he is completely still. He eats yoga, talks yoga, hears yoga, speaks yoga, sees yoga. Yoga is all of life to him.

I met my Guru for the first time when I was fourteen. Though I could not formulate it intellectually, I was aware that I had met a great being. Soon after, I left home and wandered throughout the country. I met many fully realized beings and tried to discover if any was greater than the one I had met in my boyhood. Yet many years later, I ended up with him.

There is no point in learning a few postures and then claiming to be a great yogi. You must master at least eighty-four postures, and then you must master the other three aspects of yoga— *dharana, dhyan,* and *samadhi* (concentration, meditation, and self-absorption). Only then are you worthy of being called a yogi, and if you decide to teach, you will do good work. But if you happen to go bankrupt in your business or if you flunk your exams and then turn to yoga to make up the loss, you won't get very far.

I read a story about a tiger who became an apostle of nonviolence. As the tiger aged, he lost the strength of his youth and had to drag his body around painfully. He began to wonder how to make his livelihood. Now that he was too slow to catch an animal on the run, the poor fellow found himself starving. So the tiger decided to become nonviolent, or at least to make a pretense of nonviolence. He was so meticulous that when he moved he would blow on the earth to make sure that no insects were crushed under his heel. With every breath he kept muttering. "Sri Ram, Jay Ram, Jay Jay Ram," so that people would take him for a real *babaji*, a renunciant. He would look to one side and then to the other, take a step, and utter, "Sri Ram, Jay Ram," then take a second step and look to see if anyone was around to hear him. If there were, he would repeat his phrase a little louder.

A monkey sitting in a tree watched the tiger very closely thinking, "At last, here is a true saint who has absorbed nonviolence into his very being." He was impressed by the way the tiger looked carefully at the ground before taking a step and with the tiger's devoted utterance of "Sri Ram." After awhile, the monkey came down from the tree and stood at a respectful distance from the tiger. He said, "Sir, who are you? How has this change occurred, and where are you going?"

The tiger answered, "Dear fellow, when I look back on my life, I am filled with remorse. I misled so many creatures, teaching them how to hunt other creatures and catch them and eat them up. Because I am ashamed of what I have been, I have decided to turn over a new leaf and become an initiate of nonviolence. Now I am so scrupulous about preserving life that I would blow away the tiniest ant that came in my way, and I would not take one step without uttering 'Sri Ram.'"

The monkey was so moved that he threw himself down before the tiger, certain that he had finally encountered a truly nonviolent being. The moment the monkey's head was on the ground, the tiger grabbed it, and the monkey was in a fix. "I have been caught in the trap of nonviolence," he thought. "If I had not gone so close to this Yogiraj, I wouldn't have gotten in trouble."

Suddenly, the monkey had an idea. He began to laugh wildly, uproariously. The more he laughed, the more astounded the tiger became, until finally he said, "Brother, why are you laughing?"

The monkey answered, "Tiger dear, though I am caught in the jaws of death, I am laughing because I know astrology. This is the most auspicious hour for dying. Anyone who dies right now will go straight to heaven. It's absolutely guaranteed, and that's why I'm laughing."

The tiger did not want to miss his chance to go to heaven. In his confusion he opened his mouth widely, and the monkey escaped. When he had climbed to a safe place in a tree, the monkey began to weep and lament loudly, "O Lord, what is happening to your world?"

Now the apostle of nonviolence was even more taken aback. "What a strange fellow. When he should have wept he laughed, and now that he should laugh, he is weeping. Brother, your behavior is most irrational. I don't begrudge you your escape, but now that you are safe at the top of a tree, why are you weeping?"

The monkey answered, "Brother, when I was between your teeth, I began to laugh because I wanted to escape your fangs, but now that I am on top of a tree I'm weeping because I see that apostles of nonviolence, such as you, are the greatest danger to this world. I am praying to God to do something about it."

Many teachers grab innocent necks in the name of nonviolence; so it's natural for the monkey to be frightened and to lament. However, I can assure you that true yogis, truly enlightened beings, and true devotees will always exist in God's world, though their number may vary from time to time. In our country it is a tradition that a Guru, before accepting anyone as his disciple, test him thoroughly and keep on testing him for a long period of time. Only after the Guru has become convinced of a disciple's credentials does he transmit a portion of his divinity to him. Likewise, a disciple should be very careful before accepting his Guru. He should keep company with him long enough to know whether he can deliver the goods or not and whether there is any real love in him. Accepting a Guru is not like seeing the title of the latest movie and rushing off to the theater to see it. Yoga is supposed to bring supreme peace, and anyone who claims to be a yogi should embody that peace in his person. You yourself should be able to feel it. Only then should you decide if you are going to hand over your life to him.

I will tell you now what is meant by a true Siddha Guru. The first mark of a Siddha is that his sexual fluid has started to flow upward. Come what may, it will never flow downward, for it has become steady in the cerebral center. A Siddha has visited the world of the Siddhas, the world of perfected beings, and has become worthy of their grace. He has seen the supreme truth as it really is, within himself. A Siddha Guru lives in a state totally above body-consciousness and remains continually drunk on inner bliss. He is not conscious of the distinction between Guru and disciple. He is not trying to form a new sect or force any dogma down people's throats. He is not trying to enlist more and more followers. Some people think a Siddha displays miracles (*siddhis*); that is a distortion of the meaning of the word *Siddha*. To a Siddha the whole cosmos is nothing but a mass of consciousness. The forms he sees around him are only different configurations of consciousness. Why would he try to impress anybody with miracles when he considers nobody different from himself? Siddha Yoga is not simply *asanas* (postures) or *pranayama* (breathing exercises). Siddha Yoga is not something one "does." The essence of Siddha Yoga is to be received by the grace of a Siddha Guru. The true meaning of yoga is "that which reunites you with the Lord, from whom you have become separated."

Another mark of a Siddha is that he is supremely free from the pull of the senses. Nothing in this world can arouse or disturb him, for a Siddha is fulfilled within himself. A Siddha Guru does not need an army of secretaries. He doesn't seek fulfillment in any outward activity.

Guru Nanakdev used to say that some people who wash their bodies three times a day call themselves Siddhas. In that case, frogs and fish who live in water all the time would be the greatest

Siddhas. Other people claim to be Siddhas just by growing beards; in that case, goats would be the greatest Siddhas. If those who subsist entirely on milk could be Siddhas, then babies and calves would be the greatest Siddhas. Guru Nanak says that without the grace of a Siddha nothing has meaning. A Siddha manifests the power of mantra, *mantra virya*, literally the semen of a mantra. In other words, a Siddha is one who awakens the inner *shakti*. No wonder Parashiva, the Lord, says, "Such a Guru, such a Siddha, is the same as I am."

A great saint of our country, Tukaram Maharaj, has written: "A Siddha is one who by meditating on Parabrahman, the supreme reality, sees that reality within himself and thus becomes that reality; by meditating on God, he becomes God. Even gods and goddesses bow down to him."

To a Siddha, the world is not a material phenomenon, not "world," in fact, but the light of pure consciousness which shines, shimmers, and sparkles everywhere. He sees the rays of that light in children, in men and women, in animals and trees, and in himself. Though he dwells in the body, he is apart from the body. For him there is no distinction between the seer and the seen, the perceiver and the perceived; to him, matter and consciousness are only different degrees of awareness. A Siddha has merged with Parabrahman, the highest Lord, and sees the Lord everywhere; to him the world is nothing but God's playground. He does not consider anybody else inferior to him. By imparting the mantra, he does not begin to think that another person is a disciple and he is a Guru because he sees everyone as the same Lord. He revels in God's playground all the time. Tukaram says, "If you find such a Siddha, throw yourself at his feet."

Such a being, through the practice of Yoga, through philosophical or metaphysical contemplation, and through love of his Guru, has succeeded in saturating even his physical form with the power of yoga. Not only has his inner Self become one with the supreme Self, but his body is wholly conscious. You find rays of *chiti* blazing in every part of a real Guru's body. In his presence, yoga comes to you naturally, spontaneously. The rays of *chiti* emanate from him all the time and pass into spiritual seekers. Just as the clothes of a sick man are filled with germs that can be passed to anyone who touches his body or his clothes or drinks the water drunk by him, so a Guru is completely saturated with rays of *chiti*. If he were to breathe into someone's nostrils or eyes, *chiti* would pass into that person. If he were to throw his hat to someone, rays of *chiti* would pass into him.

If a Guru were to show even 50 percent of the following traits, or if not 50 percent at least 40 percent, he would be quite dependable: His body has become transmuted into pure energy; he can awaken the dormant *shakti* of a student, through *shaktipat*; he can remove all the blockages from a student's nerves, without surgery; he can open the knots in his personality; he is conscious of the truth and can transmit it directly to a disciple; he has completely mastered all the scriptures; he is established in supreme peace and experiences it without interruption; he has mastered all his sense organs—his eyes will see only if he commands them to see, his hands will move only if he commands them to move, his tongue will speak only if he commands it to speak, his mind will think only if he wants it to; he has conquered the six enemies which are lust, wrath, greed, ignorance, and so on. These are the marks of a Siddha.

A Siddha Guru is not a deceiver who cheats a disciple of his wealth. A Siddha Guru only cheats a disciple of his misery. Just as there are self-propelled boats and airplanes, the *sadhana* of a disciple becomes self-propelled once the Guru sets it going. By keeping company with a true master, you overcome bondage; you expand inwardly until you too become infinite, the supreme Lord himself. A Guru turns his disciples into *Narayan*; he makes them like God. A Guru rids a seeker of seeking and transmutes him into a Guru; he bestows guruhood on disciples. He doesn't like to keep them disciples forever. Only such a one is worthy of worship.

Because it is difficult to recognize a true Guru, it is essential for a seeker to be true as well. He should not be in a hurry to accept a Guru because taking a Guru is the most significant event in his life. Between birth and death we do many things: We grow up and get married; we have children and look after our family. But accepting a Guru and entering into the Guru-disciple relationship is the most meaningful of all events. Therefore it is not something one should do in a hurry. It is better to stay calm and make yourself a better and better disciple. I can assure you there is a world of Siddhas which I have visited, and that world is full of real Gurus. If you have become a real disciple, any one of those Gurus will come from that world and initiate you from within.

It often happens that when a person feels bored and unhappy with himself he looks around for a partner to brighten up his life. But the partner turns out to be equally self-hating, and they only wind up making each other more miserable. Before there was only one who was weeping. Now they hug each other and weep together. This should not happen between a Guru and a disciple. When you are sick of conflicts, tensions, and anxieties, you turn to a Guru in the hope that he will give you some relief. But it often happens that the Guru and his disciple hug each other and weep together in their misery. The Guru has nothing to give to the disciple, and the disciple has nothing to give to the Guru. The Guru hasn't seen Ram, and the disciple never sees Ram.

Once Alexander decided to invade India. Before setting out he went to his Guru, Aristotle, and bowed to him, saying, "Sir, I am sure I will conquer India. Is there anything I can bring you from there?"

Aristotle answered, "Bring me only a couple of Gurus who could help our people by transmitting highest philosophy to them and teaching them true yoga so that they will be able to realize God from within."

Alexander set out, and he invaded India in the area of the Punjab. But the people of the Punjab are very fierce, and they drove him away. He returned home, unable to conquer India. He couldn't even grab a Guru to take to his country.

Therefore, do not rush to accept a Guru; there is no hurry. First, find out whether a particular Guru is worthy of the title—if he has spiritual power or not—and then accept him. Always remember the inner Guru, the Guru who dwells within you forever, and he will certainly bestow his grace on you. Don't worry or be

anxious at all; when you are worthy to keep [a]
Guru, God will certainly send you one.

In my younger days I was strong and well built, and [b]
in the sufficiency of self-effort alone. I had practiced As[c]
Yoga religiously, following all its rules and disciplines. I also p[d]
ticed Hatha Yoga and spent periods of time with great Vedant[a]
teachers. I met at least sixty of the greatest teachers, and I learned
a lot from them, but I did not acquire the certainty that my inner
being had been opened. Though my body was well-shaped and
people admired my strength and beauty, though they considered
me highly realized, I always felt a lack within me. I knew that I
had not attained the highest truth, and this feeling often tormented me. It compelled me to keep wandering around on foot,
and I thought I would spend my entire life that way.

During the course of my wanderings, I came upon a saint whose
name was Zipruanna. He was the strangest of all the saints I had
met. He used to sit on heaps of rubbish in the most out-of-the-way
corners of town. He obviously neglected his body; yet his body
was so purified by the fire of yoga that the garbage he was sitting
on didn't affect him at all. On the contrary, a sweet fragrance
came from him at all times. He was very old and like a skeleton,
and he didn't have any teeth, but he was omniscient. He knew the
past, present, and future of anyone who came to see him, and he
would throw out mysterious hints, never giving a clear explanation
of anything. He hid his inner powers so well that nobody had the
slightest idea of what they were. The moment I met him he said,
"Stop this wandering and go straight to Ganeshpuri."

I was astonished. I stayed with him for three days. People used
to ask me why I kept company with such a mad, dirty old man. I
told them he wasn't crazy, we were; we appear clean on the outside, but inside we are twisted. He appeared impure on the outside, but within he was extremely pure.

I developed great love for him, and he also showered affection
on me. Once he cured my headache by licking my head with his
tongue. I followed his instruction and went straight to Ganeshpuri.

When I met my Guru Baba Nityananda for the first time, I was

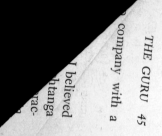

ation although I had practiced
otion and discipline. But the
Baba Nityananda caused some-
he gave me a pair of wooden
e also spoke to me. It felt as
itered my inner being. Though
rom outside, from within he was

ctrine of the sufficiency of self-
f the Guru's grace. Since then I
have emphasized it to ......   I knew sixty great teachers, but
my inner *shakti* was awakened by Nityananda alone; he was my
true Guru. The Guru has done his work if he has awakened your
inner *shakti*, but that does not mean there is no place for self-
effort. Self-effort and the Guru's grace are like the two wings of a
bird: The bird needs both to fly.

The day I met Nityananda Baba, I realized the wisdom of the
Upanishadic seers who said, "O seeker of liberation, go to a
master who is well versed in all the scriptures (*shrotriya*) and who
also has had a direct experience of God (*brahmanishtha*)."

There are many scriptures, and the Guru has to read them all.
If he only had himself to take care of, it wouldn't be necessary,
but he has to guide so many different sorts of people. One who is
shrotriya can guide diverse seekers perfectly. A Guru must not
only know the religious and philosophical truths as given in the
scriptures, but he must also be well versed in many worldly arts.
In ancient times Gurus were able to ride horses and shoot as well
as perform other arts and skills. In playing the role of Guru you
have to know everything. It isn't enough to know God. If a Guru
has to guide seekers living in the world, he must be familiar with
their pleasures and pains, with their joys and sorrows, and with
the various problems which afflict them. A true Guru is master of
all trades, but even that is not enough.

The Guru must also have the quality of *brahmanishtha*. He
must have had a direct experience of God; he must have seen God
as you and I see any object in the outer world. Only such a one
can be worthy to be a Guru. Such a Guru is like God. There is

no difference between him and the divine being. He has merged his own individuality into the absolute and become one with it. He is forever free from the chains of limited existence and limited knowledge. Such Gurus are badly needed in the world.

We should honor such a Guru with the greatest devotion and reverence because he works within us, transforming us into divine beings. The Guru within is much closer than any outer teacher. After receiving a Guru's *shakti*, you will constantly see him in meditation, in visions, and in dreams. The greater your reverence, the greater your devotion, the higher you consider him to be, the more you will gain from him. If you have full devotion, reverence, and love for him, there is not the least doubt that you will receive all that the Guru has within him to give. But you must be free from affectation, hypocrisy, and pretense. Your devotion must be genuine.

When you worship the Guru, you are worshiping him for your own sake. Don't think you are doing the Guru a favor. In this context, I will narrate a short story from the great epic, the Mahabharata.

Dronacharya, a great teacher, was an expert archer, and princes used to come to his ashram to learn that skill from him. A young tribal boy, Eklavya, was very impressed by Dronacharya's ability and knowledge and asked to be accepted as a student. Dronacharya refused, but Eklavya was determined to learn from Dronacharya anyway. Every day he would come to the ashram, sit in a corner, and gaze at Dronacharya. Then he would go back to his hut and recreate in clay what he had seen in living flesh. He worked on the image of Dronacharya every day until it was finished. Then he considered it his Guru. He worshiped the statue with great love and reverence. Addressing the image, he said, "O beloved Gurudev, I am going to learn everything from you alone!" And with this firm resolution, he went into the forest and started practicing archery and meditating on the form of his Guru.

Dronacharya became active within him. The power of meditation is such that the object and the act become one. In the course of time, Eklavya learned all Dronacharya had to teach. From head to foot, he himself was transformed into Dronacharya.

One day a dog, holding a kitten between its jaws, happened to pass by. Eklavya was sitting under a tree. With his bow, he released an arrow which hit the dog between its teeth, and the kitten fell out. As a result, the dog started barking loudly and ran in the direction of Dronacharya's ashram, where all the royal students were practicing. When they saw the dog, they were amazed. Who has the skill of shooting an arrow in that manner? they wondered. Dronacharya was also amazed. He thought, "I always kept this secret to myself. How could another person learn it?" He asked his students to remove the arrow from the dog's teeth, but they could not. Then he asked them to go see if anyone with a bow and arrow was around and, if so, to bring him back.

Eklavya was relaxing comfortably under a tree when they saw him. He admitted that he had shot the arrow; so they asked him to come to the Guru.

"Who released this arrow?" Dronacharya asked.

"I did," said Eklavya.

"And who taught you?" asked Dronacharya.

"You did."

"No, I didn't. Why do you say I taught you?" Dronacharya said.

"I came to your ashram every day, and when I returned home, I worked on a statue of you. Every day I worshiped you and meditated on you. Through my worship of your form, your *shakti* revealed itself to me and started working within me. Eventually I learned everything from you."

Saying this, he bowed down to his Guru.

Dronacharya told his royal students, "The tribal boy learned this through devotion, whereas you would not be able to learn it even if I tried to teach it to you."

If such is the quality of your devotion to the Guru, you will receive his full knowledge, but the one you worship must be a perfect master. He must belong to the tradition of perfected ones, Siddhas. He must be liberated from worldly entanglements and have the power to enable his students to attain the same freedom. He should have pure love for his students and disciples and not become attached to them. He should know himself completely. If he doesn't know himself, how can he communicate any knowledge to you? If he is not liberated, how can he open the locks which imprison you?

The true Guru has fully realized God and has himself become God. Even though he appears an ordinary human being, within him divinity is revealed in its fullness. One who shouts slogans of victory to such a Guru, one who serves such a Guru, will himself become the Guru in course of time.

Somebody brought a duck to Sheik Nasrudin who cleaned it and then made a soup of it. He drank half of the soup and put the remaining half away. The next day somebody knocked at his door, and the sheik asked, "Who is it?"

"I'm the friend of the man who brought you the duck."

"All right, come in."

Nasrudin added some water to the soup and served part of it to his guest, who left after a while. Then there was another knock at the door.

"I am the friend of the friend of the man who brought you the duck."

"Come in," Nasrudin said and he added a little more water to what was left of the soup and served it to the guest. In a short while another person came along, and he too knocked.

"I am the friend of the friend of the friend of the man who brought you the duck."

By this time there was no soup left. So Nasrudin served him pure water, and his guest said, "Sheik Sahib, what kind of soup is this?"

Nasrudin answered, "Don't worry, just as you are the friend of the friend of the friend of the man who brought me the duck, this is the soup of the soup of the soup of the original soup."

So it is with many priests, teachers, and false Siddhas who are the final delusion of the soup.

Q: What does it mean to have a Guru?

long as your *shakti* is not awakened, as long as you do not feel its
Baba: To have a Guru means to be awakened from within. As
inner vibrations, you do not have a Guru; you have only seen a
Guru.

Q: Is there anything one can do to receive a Guru's grace?

Baba: All that's required is love and faith in the Guru, nothing else. Even a little love will draw the Guru's *shakti* to you. The greater the flow of love, the more the *shakti* leaps and plays inside you. One who is obsessed by women becomes like a woman; one who entertains thoughts of anger sinks into the pit of anger; one who is constantly obsessed by *maya*, illusion, falls into the trap of illusion. Likewise, Sundar the poet-saint says, "One who thinks of the Guru continually becomes like the Guru." You draw the *shakti*, the power, of one whom you love into yourself.

Q: If I let the Guru direct my life, won't it result in a weakening of my capacity for making decisions and a decline in intelligence?

Baba: I could never show my Baba Nityananda enough respect in return for what I received from him. Yet my intelligence and my capacity for decision-making didn't leave me and go to him. When you learn something from an artist or a professor, does your intelligence go over to him? It is wrong to think that by following your Guru your intellect becomes weaker. On the contrary, when the inner *shakti* awakens, your intellect acquires new strength and your mind gains new penetration.

If you surrender to the Guru, the only thing to suffer will be your shortcomings. When the river surrenders to the ocean, it becomes the ocean. When a seed loses itself in the earth, it multiplies and becomes a tree crowned with flowers and fruit. Through surrender, man does not become smaller; on the contrary, he becomes greater. Who says you cannot meet God? Remove the ego, and you have God immediately. By destroying the ego, one becomes God.

Q: Is every Guru the same as every other one in essence and development of consciousness?

Baba: All true Gurus have developed their consciousness to the same degree. The scriptures have defined the nature of the Guru at great length. The Guru is not simply a man, nor is he a deity or an incarnation or a businessman or an artist. He is just a Guru. He has completely merged himself in God so that his inner state never changes. Though his eyes are open on the outer world, his vision is really fixed within. He is addicted only to his devotion to his own Guru. Though he is a Guru himself, he is immersed all the time in devotion to his Guru. All such Gurus are in the same state. According to the Shiva Sutras, the basic philosophical text of the Kashmir school of Shaivism, a Guru is saturated with the divine power of grace. The inner essence of all true Gurus is the same. Their attainments are also the same. One who becomes a Guru by surrendering himself to his Guru is a true Guru. In his presence and by following his teaching, a disciple's Self-awareness also is unfolded.

Q: After you have found the Guru, then what?

Baba: After you have found the Guru, follow the path he has shown you and practice his teaching fully, with the aim of advancing along the path as far as you can go. However, there is an important distinction to be made. You should follow the path taught by the Guru, not imitate his ways, otherwise you will be in danger. That is why many students of Siddhas fall short in their seeking.

I read a story about Saint Makarios, a great Siddha from Greece. Because he was always immersed in ecstasy, many people began to follow him, imitating his outer ways without paying much attention to his inner state or his teachings. One day Makarios was sitting with his disciples on the bank of a lake giving a lecture. While he talked, he put his hand into the water, took out some fish, and swallowed them alive. Although Makarios had swallowed only a few small fish, when his disciples saw what he had done, they fished out a few hundred of them, cooked them, spiced them, ate them, and washed down their meal with plenty of wine.

The next day the group moved on, and the disciples were very happy to be with such a wonderful master. After a while they came to another bigger lake without a single fish in it. Makarios spat out the fish he had swallowed the previous day. They were still alive, and they began to sport about in the water. The disciples tried to spit out the fish they had eaten too, but all they could bring up was their own vomit.

That is not what I mean by following a Guru. If you really want to advance along the spiritual path, you have to be firm, resolute, disciplined. A disciple must also continue to do his own work and have faith in it. Whatever your field of activity, you should stick to it and follow the Guru's teaching at the same time. You should be active, live by the fruit of your own labor as far as possible, and follow the path shown by the Guru. A disciple should forge further and further ahead on the path. He should give himself completely to the Guru and in return should become the Guru. Jnaneshwar Maharaj says, "I have been saved, I have been saved. By the grace of my Guru, I swam across to the other shore." That is what should happen. One shouldn't drown in Guru's grace but swim across with its aid. The moment you receive the touch of the Guru's *shakti*, you are saved. And it doesn't matter how much time the final realization takes; so you don't have to start counting the days.

A boy named Jabali went to his Guru and asked, "Kindly grant me the knowledge of Brahman."

The Guru answered, "Take these ten cows. When they have multiplied to one thousand, come back and I will instruct you."

Jabali took the cows into the forest and looked after them carefully, living only on their milk. At last their number had multiplied to one thousand; so he started herding them toward his Guru's ashram. Along the way an extraordinary figure rose before him and said, "O Jabali, do you know me? I am the element of earth. Your sense of smell derives from me. I am the heaviness of your body." Jabali listened and went his way.

After a while another figure stood before him. It said, "O Jabali, do you know me? I am the element of water. All of your bodily fluids, including your blood, are derived from me. I am your very life." Jabali listened again and went his way.

Soon a third figure loomed before him. "O Jabali, do you know me? I am the element of fire. I digest the food you eat and enable you to speak. When I cool, the world perishes. When the fire in your body cools, your body will perish."

Then a fourth figure appeared. "O Jabali, I am the element of air. I rule the beings you have encountered along the way. I am your *prana* and *apana*, the breath you inhale and exhale. I am also the wind blowing on your face."

At last a fifth figure who was hollow appeared. "O Jabali, I am space. When you strike an object, the sound produced comes from me. If I were not present in your body, the particles of flesh would huddle together and your life would end. My emptiness contains the world."

Jabali returned to his Guru. He left the herd of one thousand cows to graze before the ashram and bowed at the feet of his master, who asked, "How did you spend your days?" Jabali told his Guru all that had happened on the way back, and the Guru said, "Do you understand now that whatever exists in the body derives from one element or another, therefore none of it belongs to you? When the elements dissolve, only pure consciousness remains, which cannot be reached by imagination, intellect, or ego. Yet it lends dynamism to imagination, intellect, and ego, enabling them to function. O Jabali, God is not what the mind thinks about. God is what enables the mind to think. Meditate calmly and find out who is the witness of your mind. Meditate on the inner Self which enables the eyes to see, the ears to hear, and the nose to smell yet is beyond the reach of all these senses."

That is how the Guru instructed Jabali and Jabali became fully enlightened.

Q: To whom does the Guru give *shakti*?

Baba: The Guru gives *shakti* to a student who is willing to receive it. He doesn't decide that he is going to give it to one and not to another. That's like asking to whom the sun gives its heat. Anyone can tell you that a person who takes the trouble to go outside and stand in the sun will receive its heat, whereas if he were to keep on sitting in his house, he wouldn't receive it. The sun has no favorites. Such a thought has no meaning. If you open yourself to the Guru, the *shakti* will flow into you from him. Even if he didn't give it to you, you could draw it from him by force.

Q: Please explain what is meant by the Guru's feet.

Baba: The Guru's feet are like the foundation on which a building stands, but they should not be confused with certain physical limbs. When Jnaneshwar says, "I worshipped the Guru's feet," he is referring to something more than his physical body. The Guru is not one who talks all the time, nor is he one who teaches some kind of acrobatics in the name of yoga. The Guru is really the Lord within. In other words, the Guru is that state of profound absorption in which there is complete union with the inner Lord. The Guru's feet are *tat* and *twam* in the phrase *tat twam asi,* which means "I am that." The two syllables in *So'ham* are the actual Guru's sandals.

Yes, the Guru's physical feet are feet too, but his actual and profound feet are the two elements in *So'ham.* To worship them truly does not mean to offer him a pair of old sandals with a few flowers on them, but the moment he turns his physical face away to turn your face away from him. Awareness of one's identity with the Guru is true worship of the Guru's feet. Jnaneshwar says, "I worshiped your feet by realizing the identity of myself with God, the identity of *tat* with *twam.*"

Live continuously in this awareness and worship the internal Guru's feet. There is not much point in worshiping these physical limbs of mine. My real feet are the message: "Meditate on your self, honor and worship your Self, kneel to your Self, because your *Rama,* your Lord, dwells within you as you."

Q: What is the connection between the guide, or Guru, as we experience him within us and the actual outer Guru? Can the power and memory of Christ be the Guru within?

Baba: If you were to truly love Christ, the dormant *shakti* would easily be awakened. There is not much difference between the inner Guru and the Guru outside you in the world. Though you may appear to worship the outer Guru, the truth is that your worship is directed inward toward your own heart. Whatever you do for God, it is you who reap the harvest inside. Our Guru Gita says that in the *sahasrar*, the thousand-petaled spiritual center in the cerebrum, there is a triangle, and in the middle of that triangle lives the inner Guru. That Guru is supremely effulgent. The brilliance of his light equals a thousand outer suns; but while the light of the outer sun heats you up, the light of the inner Guru cools you.

To anyone who reaches the higher states of meditation, the inner Guru reveals himself in the form of a blue dot which we call the Blue Pearl, and it keeps vibrating all the time. When you receive the message of truth from the Guru within, you become aware that the outer Guru you have worshiped is no different from the Guru you have seen inside. The inner Guru is the same for all people of the world, regardless of their race or religion. Therefore it is right to say that Christ is seated right here as the supreme Guru within everyone.

Meditation

In ancient times a substance was said to exist called the philosopher's stone, which could transmute base metals into gold. Tukaram Maharaj, a great poet-saint of India, has written that the analogy of the philosopher's stone is inadequate to describe what a Guru does to his disciple. A philosopher's stone cannot turn base metal into another philosopher's stone; yet a Guru by his divine touch transmutes a disciple into a being just like himself. A Guru's touch is infectious, and one who receives it acquires the power of communicating that touch to others.

I have said all this in honor of my Guru, and now I welcome and honor all of you, for man is worthy of the highest honor. Every possibility exists within him before he has experienced it. The bliss which surges like a limitless ocean, the pure state of drunkenness which lies beyond all space and time, has always existed within him and is present within him now.

Most people like to see what's happening around them. They go to movies, hotels, and restaurants, but they don't care to see what lies within their own Self. It's a shame that we are so devoted to emptying our pockets and our hearts while ignoring the inner realms which could rejuvenate us if we knew of them. That is why we should meditate on the inner Self, our true reality. In a dialogue between Lord Shankara and Brahma the creator, Shankara says, "No matter how much knowledge a person has acquired, how many lectures he gives wandering from place to place, and how many books he reads or writes, no matter how many ascetic practices he follows, such as not eating or drinking, not looking up or down, not moving at all—he may become a fanatic who will refuse even the slightest whiff of fresh breeze blowing from any direction—as long as his inner *shakti* is not awakened, he cannot experience his own true reality, which is Brahman."

If you want to find permanent peace, if you want to keep happy and aware, your inner *shakti* must be awakened. God's divine light shines within everyone. Have you ever seen it? What's the point of seeing the glare of some electric light which only blinds your eyes?

If we could devote just a little time to meditation, say the time that we spend on unnecessary talk, and if, during that time, we turned our attention toward our own inner Self, with the help of a master's grace, without a doubt we would achieve something.

In this connection I am reminded of a story. One day King Sultan Mohammed was riding through his capital to find out the state of his subjects. As the king rode by a gold mine near the outskirts of the city, he saw a man sitting next to the road. Completely absorbed in his task, the man was straining the earth to get a few tiny particles of gold. His head was bent down, and he stared intently at the contents of the sieve. The earth he had strained rose beside him like a mountain. The king looked at the man and was filled with pity. He took off his precious necklace, threw it on the mound of earth, and rode away.

The next day, the king again went out for a ride through the same district. He caught sight of the same man straining the same earth through the same sieve. The king approached him and said, "Yesterday, I think you found a precious necklace that is surely valuable enough to meet your material needs for the rest of your life. Why are you still working so hard? Why don't you stop and go home and live comfortably?"

The man said to the king, "Finding a gold necklace yesterday has inspired me to work even harder because I may find something more valuable still. Yesterday I found a precious jewel, tomorrow who knows what I may find?"

That should be the seeker's attitude toward his *sadhana*. But today a seeker goes to a teacher, pays him two dollars, and receives a mantra; he gets bored with the mantra in a short while, goes to another teacher, pays him five dollars, and gets a lesson in meditation. Then he gets bored with meditation and chases after a third teacher who might give him a *yantra*, a geometrical design supposed to possess divine properties. He gazes at that stupidly for awhile and gets bored with it too. Then he puts the blame on yoga, yogis, and yogic practices and shouts at the top of his lungs that all yogis are fakes and that yoga cannot get you anywhere.

Meditation is not something new and exotic which has to be learned. We already meditate a great deal during our daily life although we are not aware of it. For instance, suppose you attend a lecture at a certain time in a distant place. You must follow directions so that you arrive there, not anywhere else. You could not do this if you did not concentrate. A reporter frequently notes down what I say when I am lecturing; he or she couldn't do that without the capacity for focusing the mind, which is just another name for meditation. Some people go to a movie, see the latest fashions on the screen, and the next morning rush to a hairdresser to get the newest hair style, then to a tailor to get new clothes made. Even that would not be possible without the capacity for meditation.

Turn this capacity inward, and meditation will come to you quite easily. I assure you, there is no real contentment in life without it. If you could find contentment through the activities of your waking hours, through eating and drinking and learning and acquiring, then you would not spend so many hours each night in sleep. Even at night you would go on eating, drinking, learning, and acquiring. Instead you want to put all this aside, retire to the darkness of your small bedroom under the warmth of a blanket, and turn off all the lights. Imagine how much greater the energy flowing into you would be if you were to go beyond the state of sleep to another state, meditation. Sages have said that meditation enables you to see the inner Self easily. We don't meditate simply to relax a little and get some peace. The Lord of yoga says, "Through meditation we reach an amazing place where the sun doesn't shed any heat, where the moon doesn't cool, where the wind doesn't blow, and where death cannot enter; where none of the miseries and calamities of our external life can penetrate." It is the place of continual bliss. If a yogi begins to live there, he becomes immortal; he has gone beyond the reach of death.

We want to escape sorrow and fear; yet we resort to means which only increase our sorrow and fear. We want peace, but we act in ways which make us more restless. Our search will succeed only if we reach the inner place through meditation.

In meditation I saw a great divinity within my own *sahasrar*, the spiritual center at the top of the head. By the grace of my Guru, by his mere touch, I saw the light of a thousand suns blazing there. But still I kept at it for a long time. Then in the inner space I heard various kinds of divine music; there is no instrumentalist, no singer there, yet I heard marvelous melodies. You can experience this easily through meditation.

It isn't hard to meditate; all you need is a genuine interest and love for it. If you turn to a Guru, relying on his help and grace, then meditation will come to you quite naturally. We find in our daily life that love, anger, and desire are activated by various stimuli. So there is no reason to believe that the inner *shakti* will not be activated if we turn to a master for support and grace. That is what the scriptures say: "Seek the help of a master who has risen completely above bodily attachment and passion."

Once, in India, a large congress of seers and sages examined the various ways of attaining God. They examined the way of action, Karma Yoga; they examined asceticism, knowledge, and pilgrimages. Finally, they concluded that God could not be attained by any of these means but only through meditation; so they meditated. They said that by meditating they were able to see the innermost reality which they could not get at even through the most subtle intellectual analysis.

When we get tired of researching the nature of reality, when we realize that our instruments cannot help us any further, meditation is the only attempt left.

Our *sadhana* is centered on meditation because the goal of meditation is to realize the supreme inner truth, but you can't have worthwhile meditation until your inner *shakti* is awakened. An aphorism in the Shiva Sutras states that if one were to acquire the power of *kundalini* one's inner being would expand infinitely and embrace the entire cosmos. As long as the awakening does not take place, one remains confined to a body which extends from head to toe and no further.

Kundalini is the creative power of the universe. It is also called Shaiva Kundalini because it is the supreme energy of Lord Shiva. Another name for this power is *chiti* because it illuminates the entire cosmos, investing it with consciousness. When *chiti* combines with the mind, it makes the mind conscious. When it combines with the sense organs, it makes the sense organs conscious. According to the sages, the goddess Chiti has brought the cosmos into being from her own Self. This universe is infinitely diverse. On the one hand, there is fire which burns, and on the other, water which cools. There is wind which moves at a terrific speed, and there is the earth which seems to be motionless. Chiti ejects a universe from her own being, with all its various shapes, diversities, and opposites. The same power becomes *prana* and *apana*, the in-breath and out-breath. It shines brilliantly in the heart. All Yoga is in the palm of *kundalini*, of *chiti-shakti*, which pervades east and west, north and south, above and below. If you were to sit in the middle of an ocean and look around, you would find water everywhere. Likewise, we sit in the middle of the ocean of *chiti*, of consciousness, and each of us is a drop in that ocean. But the special abode of *shakti-kundalini* is the base of the spinal column, *muladhar*, the very center of our body. A meditator is sometimes able to see the *shakti* within him in the form of a coiled serpent. Though it may seem limited and small, the energy of *shakti* is enough for all the purposes of creation.

Meditation is meant to awaken this power. In fact, meditation is the worship of *shakti*. When you worship her, she is propitiated and wakes up; and when she wakes up, she begins to dance. To meditate is to experience her dance within us. This awakening is possible mainly by Guru's grace. If the inner *shakti* is not awake, it would not do us much good even to live in a celestial world surrounded by gods.

I'll tell you a story. Namdev was a great saint who had realized the personal aspect of God. The Lord used to visit him quite often, and Namdev was proud to spend so much time with him. But the Lord, whose name was Pandurang, knew that though Namdev was devoted to him and saw him frequently he was not yet aware of his own true nature; his inner *shakti* had not been awakened.

At that time there were about forty great saints in Maharashtra, and they came from all walks of life. One was a tailor, another a cobbler, a third was a farmer, a fourth a barber; all the professions were represented. The saints used to assemble once a year in Pandharpur, and Lord Pandurang commanded Namdev to attend their assembly. Namdev went and sat in their midst. Each of the saints thought, "Well, here is someone who has no Guru. He can't possibly have attained truth." So they said to Namdev, "You are without a Guru; therefore you are ignorant and had better leave."

Namdev didn't like that at all. When he came home, he said to the Lord, "I didn't like those saints of yours. They said that I had no Guru, and they turned me out."

The Lord answered, "Well, what they said is true, isn't it?"

Namdev was astounded. What to do next? The Lord said, "There is a great Guru called Visoba Kechar living in a village not far from here. Why don't you go to receive instruction from him."

Namdev went to the village and asked the people, "Where does Visoba Kechar live?"

They said, "He lives in the Mahadev temple."

When Namdev reached the temple, he saw an old man lying with his legs stretched out, shoes on, and his feet propped on a statue of Lord Shiva, which people considered to be the very Lord himself. He was snoring away comfortably. Namdev decided that all *sadhus* were crazy. First the group in Pandharpur had turned him out, and now he saw another specimen with his feet and shoes propped right on the sacred image of Lord Shiva! Namdev thought, "I'd better go in and wake this fellow up and get him to remove his shoes from the Lord's image."

Namdev began to shout, "O brother! O brother! Who are you?"

The old man answered, "I am me."

"What are you doing here?"

"Can't you see I'm sleeping?"

"But you've stuck your feet right on the Lord's head. Don't you have any brains?"

The old man said, "Well, you appear to be a bright fellow. I've heard tell that you live with Lord Pandurang himself. Could you do me a favor and place my feet where the Lord is not?"

Namdev was a modern reformer, a great humanitarian, and he agreed to help him. He grabbed hold of the old man's feet and put them in a different spot, but a figure of Shiva sprang up there also. Then he moved them to a third spot, and another figure of Shiva sprang up. And then to a fourth, fifth, and sixth, but wherever the old man's feet were placed, a statue of Shiva appeared. Suddenly Namdev was jolted by the old man's *shakti* as by an electric shock. Still holding his feet, he sat reverently, plunged in amazement at this extraordinary power. The old man was a Siddha Guru, and a Siddha Guru has his own way of doing things. Then Visoba Kechar explained everything to Namdev. He awakened his *shakti* and instructed Namdev, "Don't think that the particular human form which Lord Pandurang has assumed to reveal himself to you is all there is to Lord Pandurang. He is everything you see around you and everything you don't see as well."

The *shakti* we seek to awaken is the *shakti* of Lord Pandurang which permeates everything. I can see her rays even now. A meditator should be aware of this. To awaken this *shakti*, all that is needed is Guru's grace.

In the poetry of a great Siddha, it is written: "The power of wealth is futile; the power of mind, arms, and worldly achievement is futile. There is only one thing that matters, and that is Guru's grace." Goddess Chiti sparkles within everyone, and it will not take you long to have her awake; all you need is to be aware of her.

The meditation that we practice is drawn by four horses which must be strong if the chariot is to advance powerfully. First is the object of meditation, second is mantra, third is *asana* and fourth is *pranayama*. We also sprinkle perfumed water in the meditation room because perfumes cleanse the atmosphere and are pleasing to the *prana*. The *atman* is so fond of fragrance that it stores up all the scents of the world in the *chakra* between the eyebrows. When this center opens up in meditation, we are able to smell those perfumes.

All scriptures, philosophies, sects, and religions recognize the process of meditation, whose purpose is to attain the highest peace, independent of any external or internal factors, and to remove the unreal tensions which beset our minds.

The first important question is, on what shall we meditate? Some suggest that we meditate on the mind or on certain tendencies of the mind; others suggest that we meditate on the ears, the nose, or some other part of the body. But none of these techniques enables us to meditate on God. In fact, we should meditate neither on the mind nor on the body but on the inner witness which all scriptures recognize as the supreme Lord. This inner witness is without attribute. It is aware of all thoughts rushing in the mind, all images woven by fantasy; it is aware of the pride of ego and of the decisions made by the intellect. We should meditate on this inner witness. If we were to reach it even for a moment, we would know that it has always been inside us.

The Upanishadic philosophers say, "The one your mind thinks about is not the supreme being. The supreme being, God, is the one who sets your mind to think." God is not the object of our thinking but the energy of thought itself. The Gita says, "The supreme Lord shines in all the senses. Without him no sounds could be heard, no sights seen, no words spoken. Although he shines in all the senses, he cannot be grasped by them. Although he enjoys natural qualities, he remains detached from them and is their witness."

The inner witness knows the waves of thought arising in the mind. When we sleep, we sometimes have dreams in which we perceive different worlds. What a paradox. On the one hand we say, "I sleep," and on the other hand we say, "I saw that in my dreams." Yet it is true because the inner witness does not sleep when we sleep but keeps awake and watches the events of our dreams. The same consciousness perceives all the activities of our waking state too while remaining separate from them.

This inner consciousness—inner light or inner Self—is the most miraculous of all beings, and we must learn to know him through meditation. Were we to contemplate the miracles of this being, we would become aware that physical miracles are trivial by comparison.

The Upanishads use the term *satchidananda* on which philosophers have been discoursing for centuries. *Satchidananda* consists of three elements: *sat, chit,* and *ananda. Sat* means that which is present at all times in all places and in all things. Something is *sat,* or real, because it is never absent anywhere. I exist and am real here in this place, but in Los Angeles or San Francisco at present I am not real and do not exist. Therefore, I am not *sat* which exists in all places simultaneously, including our hearts. Since we know he is there, it is quite proper to worship and meditate on *sat.*

The next element is *chit,* that which illumines everything. It is the same principle which tells me true thoughts and false thoughts and which formulates the idea, "God is within me," as well as the idea, "God is not within me." *Chiti* illuminates all things, places, and times, including our inner being. When our mind and intellect approach it through meditation, we experience it as supreme bliss, *ananda.* Therefore we meditate on the *Self,* whose nature is *satchidananda*—being, consciousness, and bliss.

In order to know the inner witness, we also use mantra. The mantra we use most often is *Om namah shivaya,* but sometimes we also use *Guru Om* because for deep meditation the fewer the letters in a mantra the better. A seer explained the meaning of *Om namah shivaya* in the following Sanskrit passage: *"Om namah shivaya gurave satchidananda murtaye, nisprapanchaya shantaya, niralambaya tejase." Om namah shivaya:* I bow to Shiva who is the supreme Guru of the world. As we meditate more and more, this Guru reveals himself to us in our meditation, in the *sahasrar,* or thousand-petaled lotus at the crown of the head. His form is *satchidananda*—being, consciousness, and bliss. *Nisprapanchaya:* in whom there is no phenomenal consciousness; who is supremely tranquil, serene, pulsing within as supreme light. We reach this being through *japa*, repetition of mantra, which I will describe more fully in chapter 5.

The third aspect of meditation is *asana*, the sitting position, and it has great importance. There are many different *asanas*, or postures, but the main ones are *siddhasana*, perfect posture, *padmasana*, lotus posture, and *sukasana*, easy posture. If one could sit still in the lotus position for one and one-half hours, all the seventy-two thousand nerves, or *nadis*, in the body would be purified. Shaivite philosophy says that one who has mastered an *asana* will taste nectar within him.

The main requirement of *asana* is that the back, the spine, be held upright. When the spine is held upright, the mind steadies itself in the heart. The best position for meditation is to sit straight up, but if you can't do that, when you are at home you can stretch yourself out flat in the corpse pose and meditate that way.

The fourth aspect of meditation is *pranayama*, or breathing. People exhaust themselves with all kinds of breathing techniques, but Shaivite philosophy says, "Don't practice methods of breathing. *Pranayama*, or right breathing, will occur spontaneously." As your mind clings to the mantra and dives inward toward the Self, your *asana* becomes steady; as your *asana* becomes steady, your *prana*, or breathing, also becomes steady. Your long breaths shorten; sometimes they stop and then start moving again as your breathing adapts itself to mantra repetition. This spontaneous *pranayama* does not require practice.

Meanwhile we should remember that the *atman*, the Self, is not something to be obtained. We already have it. All we need to do is experience the peace we already have.

One day a washerman took his donkeys to the forest to graze. While he was there, he came upon a lion cub and brought it home with him. The cub grew up along with the washerman's donkeys and learned to repeat the donkey mantra—hee-haw, hee-haw. He played with the donkeys, ate and drank with them, and carried dirty laundry with them. Time passed, and the lion cub grew up. He became a friend of donkeys and thought that he too was a donkey, sharing their ways.

One day he was grazing on the bank of a river with his donkey brothers when another lion came along to drink from the same river. While the lion was drinking, he caught sight of the young lion among the donkeys. He heard the young lion bray like a donkey and saw him graze like a donkey. Shocked to see his brother in such a pitiful state, the old lion moved closer and said, "Brother, what are you up to?"

"I am with my other brothers."

"Your brothers? They are donkeys and you are a lion. How can you call them brothers? Come with me and look into the water. Look at your reflection and look at my reflection, and see if there is anything similar between us. Now tell me who is your brother, me or those donkeys? Stop going hee-haw and start roaring."

The cub began to roar, all the donkeys ran away, and both lions went off freely into the forest. The young lion had been a beast of burden, and now he was king of the wilds. In fact, he had never really been a donkey, but he had acted like one and thought he was one.

We find ourselves in that situation. We are not donkeys, but we have come to act and feel like donkeys. If we could experience our true Self, we would know that we are lions.

Be aware of your ideal nature. You never became small but only believe that you are small. Discard this belief. Shaivite philosophy says that *chiti*, or universal consciousness, contracted into a bound form. That is how the illusion of a donkey was born. Just as *chiti* descended from its higher form and became a donkey by living with donkeys, likewise by keeping company with a lion instead of donkeys you can reverse the process. Only our self-knowledge has to be changed. We never became donkeys, and we never can become donkeys.

Each morning we sing a prayer, "Jyota se jyota jagavo," in which a devotee prays to the Guru who is purest light and says, "Kindle my flame with your flame." In the second stanza the devotee sings, "I am your child who has come to beg the gift of light from you. Please reveal the inner light to me. I bow my head." Bowing your head means that you have renounced ego, the cause of our greatest pain. Ego does not let the inner *shakti* blaze but stands as an impenetrable wall between a seeker and his Guru. Although ego is not concrete but a subtle and very thin veil between the individual and his Lord, the indwelling God, it is enormously powerful. Ego has turned light into dark and has reduced the stature of the divine being to a limited, conditioned individual. Ego blinds us to the all-pervasiveness of the inner principle. Wherever we go, ego dogs our steps like a shadow. If you go to a Guru, ego bars the way. If you go to a temple to worship God, ego bars the way. Even when you want to sleep, the ego stands between you and sleep. Therefore, the devotee sings, "I bow my head," which means, "I give up my ego. I wave lights to you. Please shower the nectar of love into my heart."

According to our scripture, the world is very old. Since it began, we are born and we die, we are born and we die. The cycle of birth and death resembles the cycle of sleep and waking. Though ages have passed, the inner *shakti* sleeps on. "O Sadguru, kindly awaken the *shakti* so that I may surpass the cycle of birth and death, sleep and waking. There is a light which always shines within. O Sadguru, help me to see that light. Help me to hear the *mahamantra*, the great mantra, So'ham, which goes on constantly within me. If I were to hear it, I would be lost in inner ecstasy, and I would become immortal."

In the meditation which follows *kundalini* awakening, the inner music, or *nada*, of So'ham can be heard, and all a seeker needs to do is keep listening to it all the time. Nothing is higher than this *nada*. Once you begin to hear it in the spiritual center at the crown of the head, you will hear it vibrating in every particle of your body. This is the voice of God. "Bestow your grace on me so that I may hear the So'ham music," the poet says. "O Sadguru, by your grace I have become *mukta*; I have become liberated from the cycle of birth and death. I have become immortal. Now that I have received your grace, I will know death no longer. Let me take refuge at your feet."

We remember the Sadguru who grants *shaktipat* with utmost love and honor, and we don't think that we are becoming a slave to a human being. To remember the Sadguru only accelerates the yogic processes which have been activated by Guru's grace.

It is strange that when we eat, drink, and talk our minds are not filled with distracting thoughts, but when we sit for meditation, crowds of thoughts race within. After a while, a meditator gets worried and tries to wipe them away, but the more he tries to push these thoughts out of his mind, the more they pour back and fill his mind again. In my opinion, you are not meditating when you do this; you are only trying to eliminate thinking from your mind. When a thought appears on the inner screen during meditation, don't try to wipe it away. Instead, consider every thought and idea to be no different from your goal, which is God. Modern research may split the mind into different faculties, but the mind is nothing but *chiti*, consciousness.

If the mind were trivial, how could it create one universe after another at such fantastic speed? If the mind were inert matter, how could it give rise to the infinite forms which appear within it in quick succession? The speed of your mind is many times greater than the speed of a space rocket; nothing made simply of matter could move so quickly. The nature of the mind is to keep on creating endless universes; how can you erase all of them? You can't. If you erase one, another will appear. If you erase the second, a third will appear. Sages have said that the mind is not what you ordinarily understand by the limited term *mind*. The mind is not matter; it is not a narrow restricted force. To achieve the purposes of the inner Self, Chiti Bhagavan, the goddess of consciousness, Kundalini herself, has become the mind. The mind is simply consciousness in a contracted form which expands once more through meditation and becomes *chiti*.

A good way to meditate is to watch these infinite forms which are thrown up by the mind, regarding them only as the play of *chiti*, the play of inner consciousness. When we sit for meditation, we should not expect anything to happen. We should rely completely on the Guru's grace. If we begin to expect something, we will be meditating only on that expectation, and our meditation will be shallow.

I'll tell you a story. A famous teacher had a large following, and one day a new student came to receive initiation from him. The teacher instructed the newcomer to sit quietly while the ceremony was prepared. When everything was ready, the Guru said, "I am going to initiate you now, and I am going to give you one instruction, which is most vital and significant. Never forget it."

The student said, "Guruji, whatever you tell me, I'll do without fail."

The teacher then told him, "When you sit to meditate, do whatever you like, but don't think about a monkey."

The disciple said, "That's simple. Why should I think about a monkey? I will think only about God. Thinking about a monkey is out of the question, you can be sure of it."

After that, he received a mantra and went to a solitary spot in the forest to meditate. He sat under a tree, closed his eyes, and began to recollect: "What did my Guru tell me? Oh, yes, don't think about a monkey!"

Immediately, a monkey came and sat in his mind. The meditator got up and faced a different direction. Again, he recollected: "What did my Guru tell me? Don't think about a monkey." And again a monkey sprang onto the screen of his mind. Again he tried, and again the monkey confronted him. At last he became frustrated. He stopped meditating, went back to his Guru, and said, "Guruji, before I received the great mantra from you, I had never thought about a monkey in my life. I hadn't even seen a monkey. But since my visit to you, I can't seem to think about anything else."

When you sit to meditate, don't impose any conditions on yourself. Whatever thought appears in your mind, let it appear. I assure you, nothing but consciousness can flash through the mind. According to Shaivite philosophy, no action or thought is without Shiva. Who, if not Shiva, could invest the mind with consciousness?

Sit calmly, repeat the mantra, and watch whatever happens in your mind, whatever flies in the inner skies. See the universe which is thrown up by your mind as Shiva. See all your mental stirrings as movements of pure consciousness, and you will get into meditation easily. If you try to empty your mind, you will never be able to meditate. Let any number of thoughts appear in the inner firmament.

Long ago I read a verse composed by a great yogi, Krishnasuta: "O my inward turning mind, where are you going? What are you thinking? Know that without the Lord behind you, without consciousness behind you, you could not go anywhere. All that appears to you is Shiva. Yet you flit from this to that and from that to this, imagining that one is better than another."

Here is the secret of initiation: Whatever you see is Shiva, whatever you hear is Shiva, whatever you touch is Shiva, whatever surrounds you is Shiva.

Vedantic philosophers have described four bodies which constitute the total human personality, one within the other. You can verify the validity of their descriptions directly through meditation. The four bodies are: the gross or physical body; the subtle body; the causal body; and the supracausal body. When by a Guru's grace the inner energy is awakened, you fall into deep spontaneous meditation without struggling to center your mind. The conscious energy working from within grabs hold of your mind and centers it properly of its own accord. As you meditate, you find yourself surrounded by a light or by a red aura the size of the body. In the glow of that red light you can see all the fluids circulating through the different nerve channels, arteries, and veins. You can see blood circulating and food being carried from one part of the body to another. You see this directly and distinctly. This light stands for the physical body and permeates all the channels within the body.

As you go deeper into meditation, you pass from the physical body into the subtle body, which is seen as a thumb-sized white light. We experience the waking state in the physical body, but we experience dreams in the subtle body. In the white light of this body we are able to see the dream world without any external light.

As you penetrate deeper, you see the third, or causal, body, which appears as a black dot the size of half a fingertip. This is not really light; it is black darkness. When you reach that state, the mind becomes totally still, and you are lost in darkness. In this body we experience the state of profound, dreamless sleep.

From the causal you pass into the supracausal, the fourth body, which is blue and is the size of a lentil seed. In this body you experience the transcendental state of consciousness. The blue spot travels at a fantastic speed and is extremely dynamic. In meditation your vision is focused upward, and you can see this fourth body, which we call the Blue Pearl, sparkling and scintillating in the *sahasrar*, the divine spiritual center in the cerebrum. We also call it the Self, or soul. In the vehicle of this Blue Pearl, or blue light, you travel from one world to another in meditation. After we die, the Blue Pearl carries us from the body to a different world.

Sometimes the Blue Pearl emerges from the eye, stands in front of the meditator, and then returns to its original place in the cerebral center. Its light is so refined, so subtle, that it passes through the eye without hurting it, nor does the eye feel its movement. The light of the Blue Pearl is so fascinating, so beautiful, so radiant, that as a meditator focuses on it he becomes lost in it. This light is the very life of man; it lends dynamism to the respiratory ryhthm. Around the Blue Pearl are spaces which sparkle with golden light, and the pearl of blue light vibrates within them. Its vibrations make it possible for the organism to function efficiently and systematically. They direct the flow of blood through the different vessels, and they help the body digest and assimilate the food it takes in.

Even this state can be reached through meditation while living a normal life. We can travel in meditation from one place to another, and all our questions about other worlds are answered. We perceive directly that the worlds described in the scriptures—the world of the moon, the world of perfected masters on the planet Jupiter (Guru), heaven and hell, and the world of departed spirits, Pitruloka—are all as real as this world. Great masters reside there although you can't see them with your physical eyes.

Whatever exists in the vast outer world exists in the inner world too, for the inner and the outer are one. The inner world may even be vaster than the outer world. In the cerebral center is a sun whose brilliance far exceeds the brilliance of the sun we know outside us. In the inner space, celestial harmonies resound. As you listen to them constantly through meditation, you become completely refreshed and regenerated. These harmonies are not created by musical instruments or by singing voices; they are self-born. All outer music is an attempt to approximate the inner harmonies, but they cannot be recreated even by the finest musicians. These harmonies are produced from the vibrations of the seed of blue light, or Blue Pearl, which I have described. As you become absorbed in listening to it, you get so high that there is no coming down. The exaltation of the inner music makes all drugs seem powerless by comparison.

As the melodies go on, you begin to hear the sound of inner thunder. Rain follows thunder in the atmosphere, and that's what happens here too. When thunder sounds in the inner spaces, a shower falls. If even one drop of that shower, which is purest elixir, reaches the tongue and travels down to the gastric fire in the solar plexus, spreading throughout the body, you experience sensations of bliss within. You experience the most intense thrill without any external touch. The elixir that rolls on the tongue from the higher center is sweeter than anything in the world.

As your eyes gaze at the blue light, they become cleansed; the ocular centers are purified. As a result you can pick up visual signals beyond the capacity of normal vision; you can see even when there is no light, for the light within the eyes is far brighter than the light outside. As your ears listen to the inner harmonies, they too are cleansed and purified so that you can pick up distant sounds. If you were to focus your attention, you could hear a conversation going on in the house next door.

When the inner nectar touches the tongue, the taste buds become extremely refined; even if you were to eat the simplest food, you would relish it as purest elixir.

The most significant of all these experiences is the vision of the Blue Pearl itself. Yoga does not mean learning a few *asanas* or giving discourses or doing a few purifactory exercises such as nasal or stomach wash. Yoga's fulfillment lies in establishing contact with the blue light, your innermost reality. After the Blue Pearl stands steady for a while, it explodes, spreading light throughout the universe. You can see it everywhere. Within that light you see your own Guru. Then you become aware of the value of a Siddha Guru, a perfected master, because you realize that his real abode was always within you in your cerebral center. Yogis can see the Blue Pearl in intense meditation by a Guru's grace. In a verse, Tukaram Maharaj has written that the master of the universe builds a tiny house for himself which is blue in color and the size of a sesame seed. The different gods, especially those constituting the trinity of Hindu mythology—Brahma, Vishnu, and Mahesh, the creator, sustainer, and destroyer—appear and disappear in the Blue Pearl.

In our tradition, much emphasis is placed on the personal aspect of the Lord. Through direct experience of the Blue Pearl, one learns the reality of the personal Lord. Within the Blue Pearl one sees other perfected masters and also the deity one has been worshiping. Yoga texts say that the Blue Pearl is the heart seed. As a seed sprouts, explodes, and grows into a huge tree, likewise, the Blue Pearl contains the entire cosmos within itself. This meditative vision is the fruit of the inner yoga which is activated by Guru's grace through awakening of *shakti*.

Q: I often feel in a hurry to have an eventful meditation. How can I get myself to take things as they come and not worry so much? As it is, my mind is often restless, which makes my meditation harder to do and less deep.

Baba: There is no need to hurry. Let meditation go at its own pace. What if you were in such a hurry about eating? But you're not the only one who is interested in speed. Everything around you goes so fast: trains, automobiles, airplanes. I wonder what people gain by rushing around so madly. No matter how fast they go, anxiety keeps up with them. So it's not your fault if you want to go fast in meditation too, but meditation is meant for a patient, steady mind. Meditation means that you apply brakes to your mind. It doesn't mean to take the brakes off and let your mind race around at top speed.

Q: Instead of meditating with closed eyes, is not meditation better if one looks at the beauty of nature, the sky, trees?

Baba: To look at the world with understanding in your eyes is an excellent form of meditation, for the Self pervades everything. Kabir speaks of "seeing in meditation." In fact, sahaj samadhi, or spontaneous samadhi, is the best and highest meditation. Wherever you look, you see not only things but the spirit which animates them. Because we do not always understand this, we close our eyes for a while. To see Self in stones, trees, and space is the meditation of the high ones. Whatever and wherever you see, you see God. Whatever you eat and drink is an offering to him. Whatever you speak is his mantra. It is the Self that is eating, drinking, and seeing. The Self is in the self. O supreme conscious Rudra, you are man and woman. I bow to you. Rudra is the sun, Rudra is the light, Rudra is all. You should be the same within and without. If you have seen within, then the same will appear outside also.

Q: How long a time must one meditate each day to secure the benefit of meditation?

Baba: An hour or an hour and a quarter every day is enough. If you want to meditate more than that, you will need strength to bear the impact of it. For that, you have to be very disciplined in your eating. It doesn't matter if it takes a long time; the best is to go slowly and steadily. Once the shakti has awakened, it keeps doing its work within you. Sometimes you may be aware of it, other times not. No matter what you are doing, whether driving your car or working at your office, the shakti penetrates every element of your being.

If you can get up early, morning is the best time to meditate.

But if you can't, you can meditate before going to sleep. Have a light dinner and then, before going to sleep, lie down and get into meditation. The meditation will last throughout your sleep.

Q: How do I overcome feelings of unworthiness and inadequacy that come during meditation?

Baba: Don't attach any importance to these feelings. You are not your feelings; you are the place where feelings arise. Just as in the upper spaces clouds appear and vanish, in the space of the heart, endless feelings and thoughts rise and set. Why should you attach any special importance to them?

Ignore the clouds and look for the sun in their midst. There are so many things around me here. There is no need to remove them all in order to meet me. Similarly look for the light among the clouds. As you concentrate on the light, your mind also will become peaceful.

While meditating, you should let go of your faults. Suppose I feel angry this evening and then sit for meditation the next morning; there should be no trace of that anger left in me. I can honor myself and meditation will come. Just as during sleep one sleeps and does nothing else, while meditating, that's all you should do.

Don't be self-conscious about your weaknesses. Attachment and hatred may be there still, but many good qualities are also present. The point is not to honor yourself for your faults but for your good qualities.

Don't let your price fall in the market by keeping alive the memory of your faults, attachments, and hatreds. Depending on your temperament, attachment and negative feelings may persist for quite some time. Nonetheless you should keep on cultivating the good qualities. Hatred and attachment don't last; so why should your thoughts about them last? If in one's life some painful event has taken place, the mark of a wise man is that he doesn't preserve the pain in his thoughts but forgets about it very soon.

Q: Is it ever permissible for a disciple to smoke ganja and hashish to help his meditation?

Baba: If ganja and hashish could help meditation, then why meditate at all? Why not simply depend on ganja and hasish? Kabir says that one who is addicted to drugs and intoxicants cannot complete his *sadhana* of meditation. Meditation affects extremely refined sensory nerves for which drugs, forbidden by the scriptures, are much too strong. Those nerves cannot even bear strong coffee. Furthermore, meditation is more intoxicating than drugs could ever be. Even if you got high on ganja, you wouldn't get very high; and when the effect wore off, you would really come down, sometimes lower than before. To get high again, you would have to use ganja again; otherwise you might not be able to bear your own company.

Meditation is far more potent than ganja, but first you have to give up drugs completely. There are no "downs" in meditation, only "ups," because the "high" of meditation will never desert you. It keeps getting stronger and stronger, so powerful is the inner intoxicant. No drug, however potent, can influence a real meditator. It is said that Mira was given poison to drink; yet it caused her no harm, for she was under the influence of a far mightier "poison"—the ecstasy and nectar of her love for Krishna. I am not speaking of any miracle or *siddhi*; this happens naturally to one who is divinely intoxicated. Therefore, meditate with love and interest. Don't seek the aid of drugs; they will dull the refined sensory nerves in your brain. Those who meditate with the aid of drugs always remain insecure and dissatisfied.

Q: Is Shiva the same as God?

Baba: You can use any name. Shiva, Brahma, or Vishnu all refer to the same reality: Parashiva, the transcendental, highest being. When he creates, he is called Brahma; when he sustains, he is called Vishnu; when he destroys all that is evil, he is called Shiva.

The Guru is also given these three names. The Guru is Brahma because he creates a new universe of knowledge in his disciple. He is Vishnu because he sustains it. He is Shiva because he destroys all that is negative and harmful in his disciple.

Mantra: Language
As God

Mantra is *Maheshwara*, the great Lord, the all-pervasive inner being. It is at the root of everything we do in this world—our practical dealings, devotion, yoga, knowledge, research into spiritual matters.

The yoga of mantra is complete in itself and has two aspects. The first, *swadhyaya*, is literally the study of your own inner Self. It also means chanting. In the morning at our ashram, at retreats, and in our homes we recite the Guru Gita, a hymn to the Guru, which is also a philosophical poem describing the nature of the inner Self. The second aspect of mantra yoga is *ishwar pranidhan* which means surrendering yourself to the Lord in every possible way.

Your spiritual and worldly lives are possible because of language, that is, words and sounds. The letters of the alphabet combine into words, and the words combine into sentences which express the meanings we need to function in our daily life. What a sentence is going to achieve depends on the set of meanings it conveys. Language comes from God. A verse says that God originally manifested himself as sound, or language. The mantra too is language, a combination of letters.

But is mantra an ordinary combination of letters or something more? It has been said that the mantra is the Lord, the highest being. To understand this, you must also understand the secret of mantra realization which is that the mantra, one who repeats the mantra, and the deity toward whom the mantra is directed are not separate from one another. They are one. Unless we experience this truth, the full power of mantra will elude us.

Language has tremendous power. A word, which we may call a mantra, can make you aware of something which exists at a great distance. If we use the mantra *Washington,* a worldly mantra, the image of the city is conjured up in our mind although we may be thousands of miles away from Washington. The same is true of a spiritual word or mantra; it enables us to realize the Lord. We use a mantra for *shaktipat;* through it, the Guru enters a disciple. The mantra that is quite often used is *Guru Om, Guru Om, Guru Om.*

A poet-saint commenting on the misuse of mantra has said, "Everybody repeats the name of Rama, including cheats, thieves, and priests." But great devotees such as Prahlad and Dhruva repeated Rama's name differently because they were redeemed by it. How did these great devotees realize the power of mantra? The answer is found in a verse of the Shiva Sutras: "Unless you are aware that the goal or deity of your mantra is your own inner Self, the supreme Lord, you cannot experience the full power of mantra, no matter how often you repeat it. Only if the goal of mantra is present in your mind will it bear fruit quickly. Otherwise, it will not bear fruit at all."

Another great saint, Eknath Maharaj, has written, "Have the name on your lips and liberation in your hand."

The fact is that every word and every single letter is a mantra whether we use it in our worldly or in our spiritual life. If while talking with a friend we become angry with him and shout, "Get out of here!" our friend goes away. Later we may feel remorse and say, "I am sorry, I love you; I didn't mean to offend you," and our friend becomes reconciled to us once again. Such is the power of a worldly mantra.

Om is the primal word uttered in the beginning of the universe. It is the sound from which everything else has emanated. *So'ham* is derived from *Om,* and so is everything else in this world. Mantra, the word which was in the beginning, is echoed in every single thing including ourselves, but we are not aware of it.

Take, for instance, flowing water. When water flows, it makes a murmuring sound which is its spiritual language, or mantra. It seems to remember God with that sound. The rustling of wind is also mantra; by rustling, the wind remembers its creator. When we walk on the earth, our footsteps produce sound, and that is the mantra which the earth repeats all the time to thank its creator. Space constantly reverberates with sound. I have read the life stories of many saints; quite frequently they heard a voice descending from space, the voice of the heavens, carrying a message for them.

Kabir, the great poet, says, "The Guru awakened me within by imparting just one word." Because we are not aware of the true nature of language and of mantra, we have split into different sects and cults, each claiming a mantra for his cult, and we go on fighting to no purpose whatever. Though the globe has been divided into fragments which we call India and Europe, America and Pakistan, the fact is they are parts of the same earth. The water I drank in India is the same as the water I drink in America. We eat the same food, our clothes are made of the same cotton, our language also refers to the same objects. I may use the word *jala* for what you call "water," but the difference is in the language, not in the object denoted by it.

Our concern should not only be with language but with meaning. Since every word has its effect instantaneously, why shouldn't a holy word have its effect instantaneously too? The answer is that we accept a swear word and believe in its meaning while we do not believe in the meaning of a holy word.

In India, we hold ceremonies at which ritual mantras are recited. The priests recite the mantra, and we repeat it with them. One day someone happened to pass by a place where a ritual was being held. He heard the priests uttering mantras, and he asked, "What do you ever get with all this babble which doesn't mean a thing?"

The mantra priest was very clever, and he answered, "You stupid ass, get out of here!" The moment the fellow heard himself spoken to this way his mouth fell open, his hair bristled, and his body started shaking. The priest asked, "Brother, what is happening?"

The fellow replied, "You claim to be a priest, yet you speak so insultingly."

The priest said, "Well, look at this. I used just one phrase, a swear word, and it had such an impact on you. What makes you think that these holy words are without effect?"

I read a verse which says, "Mantra is true, worship is true, and God is true. You will realize their truth when you yourself become true." When you accept the truth of God, of mantra, and of yourself, poison turns into nectar.

The mantra is always obtained from the mantra seer, whom we call the Guru. To be invested with consciousness, a mantra must be alive. Therefore it should be taken from one who has himself fully realized its power.

A mantra seer is one who received the mantra from his Guru and has practiced it intensely. As a result, the mantra has passed within him from the physical level of speech to the subtle, causal, and supracausal levels. All the parts of his being are cleansed and purified by the mantra, enabling him to have a vision of the Blue Pearl, which is the supreme witness of the mantra he practices.

When you receive a mantra from such a one, it is conscious and living. It carries the power of the one from whom you receive it. It will bear fruit in you.

Mirabai, a queen in our country, was a great devotee of Krishna. Every morning she would put on anklets and dance in ecstasy, singing, "Radha Krishna, Gopal Krishna, Radha Krishna, Gopal Krishna, Radha Krishna, Gopal Krishna." The royal family did not like this behavior because they were intoxicated with power and wealth. They thought it was below their dignity for one of their ladies to utter Krishna's name although they never thought it below their dignity to use the foulest language whenever they felt like it. They tried to argue with her, but she wouldn't listen because she had realized Krishna within herself. So they gave her poison, and she drank it, singing the name of Krishna. The poison turned into nectar; it would not kill her.

The name has tremendous power. It is divine yoga. Whatever people want to achieve, they can do so by repeating the name. They can get all the power they are seeking.

In my book, *Play of Consciousness*, I describe the four bodies of man. Corresponding to those four bodies are four tongues, or four levels of speech; your mantra must pass from one level to another. In the initial stage we repeat the mantra with our lips or with the physical tongue, but if our mantra just remains there, it will not bear much fruit. It must pass to a lower tongue, to the subtler levels of speech.

First you repeat the mantra on the tip of your tongue, and it vibrates there for a while. If you do it with sufficient reverence and love, it will quickly pass to the throat center, the next level.

Once the mantra passes from the tip of the tongue to the throat center, it passes from the physical body to the subtle body, from the physical tongue to the subtle tongue, from *vaikhari* (the physical level of speech) to *madhyama* (the subtle level of speech). As the mantra descends, its power increases. The fruit or reward which you may get by repeating the mantra on the tip of the physical tongue one hundred thousand times is the same as repeating it just once in the throat center. If your mantra is *Om namah Shivaya*, you will feel its vibrations in the throat center without any response from the tip of the tongue. The mantra will begin to fill you with gladness and make you more conscious. Your intellect will also be refined; you will begin to understand things, have new insights.

When the mantra reaches the throat center, you acquire a marvelous healing power. However, you must not get swept off your feet by these minor miraculous powers; if you do, further progress will be impeded. Swami Ram Tirth says that a *siddhi*, a psychic power, is a terrible enchantress. My Baba, my Guru, had a mountain of *siddhis*, but he never touched it although all *siddhis*, all powers, worked for him on their own. I never touch any of these miraculous powers either.

Once I read a story about a princess who was an extraordinary runner. When she was of marriageable age, she laid down the condition that anyone who wanted to marry her had to run against her in a foot race. If he won, she would accept him as her husband. But anyone who lost would have to serve as her slave for the rest of his life. Many proud princes came to race with her, and every one of them lost. Turned into slaves, some would sweep her floors, others would fan her, and still others would cook her food. One day a particularly clever prince decided to race the princess. He was dead serious about it because he really longed to marry her and to release all the princes who were in servitude. So he went to his Guru and asked for advice. The race was to cover three miles. The Guru said, "I'll tell you a trick. Make twenty-five gold bricks, and lay them a furlong apart along the course of the race."

In the morning the race started. At first the princess was ahead, but when she reached the end of a furlong, she saw the first gold brick and paused to pick it up. Meanwhile, the prince forged ahead. Again she ran fast and left the prince behind; but at the end of another furlong, she saw the second gold brick and paused to pick it up. This went on, and soon the prince left her far behind. When the princess reached the finish line, she accepted defeat and agreed to marry the prince who got his gold bricks back and the princess for his wife. He also freed all the other princes.

One who is running a race to reach the Lord should not let his attention be distracted by gold bricks along the path, for then he might never reach his destination because of the tremendous load on his back.

When the mantra descends to the second level in the throat, various powers are manifested. For example, whatever you utter turns out to be true. Also, you really begin to enjoy the name. It becomes so enjoyable that you like to repeat it all the time, while you're working or playing with your children or talking to your mate.

Then the name descends from the throat center to the heart center which is the third, or causal, level of speech. The deeper *japa* goes, the more powerful it becomes. I said that one repetition in the throat center is equal to one hundred thousand repetitions on the tip of the tongue, but one repetition in the heart center is equivalent to one hundred thousand repetitions in the throat center. You begin to go into a state of *tandra,* or higher consciousness, and have true visions of gods and goddesses; you also see the deity of the mantra. You can see past and future, but don't take any interest in them because your interest is focused on the mantra itself. You can feel the vibrations of the mantra in all the centers. When a physical nerve vibrates, you feel it without any doubt. Similarly, you will know when the mantra begins to vibrate in the heart center.

From the heart center, the mantra descends to the navel center, which is the fourth level of speech, the supracausal level. Here you have beatific visions. You become aware of the true nature of the universe, and you see God. It's difficult to say what wishes God will grant to someone who has reached this plane. He could be granted the wish of poetic power, or he could be granted the wish of saying something which is bound to come true. That is the mystery of the mantra. Furthermore, when the mantra begins to vibrate in the navel center, you can hear it going on within even when you are asleep.

There is a special room in my ashram near Bombay which I always keep locked. It is the room where I did *japa* and meditated for a long time when my Guru was in his physical form. As a result of my intense *japa*, I had many experiences. That's why the mantra I give is able to awaken the dormant *shakti* of a devotee. One day a high Indian civil service officer whose name was Dallal began to express skepticism about the power of mantra. I said, "Why are you talking so much? I have a special room where I'll let you sit. I won't give you a mantra, but if you spend some time in that room, you'll hear every single atom in it uttering the mantra."

After he had been sitting there for a while, he began to hear *Om namah Shivaya* coming from every direction, even from the walls. He broke into a sweat and rushed out of the room, crying, "O Muktananda Swami, O Muktananda Swami."

I said, "Dallal sahib, what has happened?"

He said, "Well, the most amazing thing. I heard your walls saying the mantra, and now I can't get rid of it. I hear the mantra repeating itself even here. It's coming from my right arm, from my left arm; it's coming from everywhere."

Such is the power of mantra. Any object you strike will produce a sound, and that sound is its mantra. Therefore, keep repeating your mantra without interruption. It is a simple, easy, and natural yoga which you can combine with your daily commitments. This yoga will fill you with peace, joy, love, and bliss. Eknath Maharaj used to sing, "Why don't you repeat it with one-pointed devotion? It will explode in your heart and reveal the bliss which lies dormant there." As you repeat the mantra, you will begin to hear the true vibration *Om, Om, Om* at the source of the mind.

Just as worldly mantras bear fruit in your worldly life, spiritual mantras are bound to bear fruit in your spiritual life, for mantra is absolutely true. Therefore, keep repeating it, knowing that the mantra, you who are reciting the mantra, and the lord or deity of the mantra are one.

A poet has given expression to the power of mantra. He tells how Radha, the supreme beloved of Krishna, used to repeat "Krishna, Krishna, Krishna" all the time. She became so completely absorbed in Krishna while repeating his name that she began to ask her companions, "Where is Radha? Where is Radha?"

In our daily practice we generally use three mantras. First, we repeat *Om namah Shivaya* at the beginning of meditation, then *Guru Om.* But the underlying mantra of the Siddha tradition is different from these two. Then why should we repeat them? There is a secret behind the mantra *Om namah Shivaya,* which is called *panchakshari,* or the five-lettered mantra. This mantra is repeated to cleanse the body which is made up of the five principle elements. If the body and mind are not pure, spiritual practices are of little use. After repeating these mantras for some time, the underlying spontaneous mantra of the Siddha tradition, *So'ham,* is initiated into your ear. The Siddhas residing in *Siddhaloka* repeat this spontaneous mantra without stop, thereby remaining in the state of Siddhahood.

In India all Siddhas and religious leaders, whether they are Jains or Sufis, use mantras as a vehicle to convey their *shakti,* or energy, into their disciple. But the true Siddha mantra, *So'ham,* is unique because it is not man-made. Although the mantra *Om namah Shivaya* was composed by Saint Markandeva, and the mantra *Guru Om* by Basveshwara, the Siddha mantra is natural and was not composed by anyone. That is why this ultimate mantra is not given indiscriminately but only according to the fitness of the student or disciple. Otherwise the value of the mantra would not be manifest. The mantra of which I speak goes on spontaneously in all living creatures. In the beginning it was imparted by the Lord himself, but then it was forgotten and now must be initiated once again by the Guru or master.

In Vedic literature, the fetus is said to receive knowledge of the past and future in the seventh month. It remembers the sufferings of its previous lives and learns of the suffering to come. It becomes restless and begins to kick and move about, but wherever it moves, the heat and secretions of the surrounding internal organs press against it, causing it to feel pain. A description of these effects is found in the Garbhopanishad which is part of the Veda. The supreme Lord takes pity on the child's suffering. The Lord has been seated all along in the mother's heart and doesn't have to come from Kailas or Vaikuntha. From his seat in the heart, he instructs the child, "Why do you move about unnecessarily? Sit peacefully in one place, remember God, and repeat the mantra *So'ham, So'ham, So'ham.*" For all of us, therefore, the supreme Lord himself was the Guru in the beginning. Many learned people don't know this simple truth though they talk about mantras and initiation. Once I met a scholarly master who said, "You tell me that God is your Guru. But when did he initiate you, and when did you receive a mantra from him?" I told him to read the Garhopanishad, and he would know what I meant. After that he wrote me a long letter saying that in all of India no one else had given him a proper explanation of this passage.

God initiated us with the *So'ham* mantra when we were in the uterus of our mother. At the end of the ninth month, a vital air called the *prabhanjana vayu* (the same vital air which consumes the entire universe in the process of dissolution) projects us out into the world. The shock of this experience is so great that as soon as we emerge we start crying, *"Ko'ham, Ko'ham, Ko'ham:* Who am I? Who am I?" forgetting the underlying mantra we learned in the womb. Later, if we meet a mantra seer, he reminds us of what the primal Guru had taught us before birth.

According to the Upanishads, when we inhale, the first part of the mantra, *So*, is pronounced, and when we exhale, the second part, *ham*, is pronounced. Thus the mantra goes on spontaneously in each and every one of us, with no effort of will. Simply breathe naturally and you will hear *So* when you inhale and *ham* when you exhale. The mantra also speaks its own natural language. The letter *So* denotes the supreme Lord, source of all religions and philosophies; the exhaled *ham* denotes the "I", thereby establishing an identity between the supreme Self and the individual soul.

The *So'ham* mantra has nothing to do with religions, casts, colors, or creeds. It belongs neither to the Hindu nor to the Christian. Sit silently for fifteen minutes in a corner, and listen to your breath filling and emptying your lungs. You will know your natural mantra and experience the result of its repetition.

It is our nature constantly to repeat one mantra or another. Can you think anything at all without a combination of subtle letters? You experience fear, hatred, pleasure, or pain according to the nature of the inner mantra. The Lord whose body is the universe appears in the form of sound. By indwelling within us, he gives us different kinds of experience through his subtle mantra.

The letters of the alphabet are extremely powerful. If even one letter is missing, the meaning of a word and the experience it imparts to us may change completely. *So'ham* too is so powerful that it awakens the inner *kundalini* immediately. Jnaneshawar Maharaj writes, "As soon as I approached the mantra *So'ham*, I entered the sleep state." Therefore in all your activities, all the time, repeat the mantra *So'ham*, *So'ham*, *So'ham*. Try it. Inhale with *So* and hold the breath inside. Feel the experience it gives. Then exhale with *ham* and feel that experience.

And yet, to tell the truth, we don't really need to repeat *So'ham*, or anything else for that matter, for we ourselves embody its repetition. How can we attain something new through *So'ham* when we have already attained it? *We are that*. Man is so forgetful; the scriptures and the saints are tired of pointing out his fundamental error.

One day the sun went out along a highway and met many people who asked him, "O sun, where are you going?"

The scorching sun answered, "I am afflicted with cold. If somewhere I could find some heat, I would feel much better."

The moon too came along the highway, and people asked, "Moon where are you going?"

The moon answered, "I am afflicted with heat. If somewhere I could find some cold, I would be so thankful."

Doctors tied a delerious man to a cot, and he shouted, "Help! They have tied me to a cot. I want to go home." But he was in his home all along. Just the sun went out in search of heat, and the moon in search of cold, the deluded man searched for his own home.

We are deluded in the same way, searching for our own Self. We meditate and try different practices. Yet Lord Sri Krishna says in the Gita, "O Arjuna, the Lord is right within you, not somewhere else, and he doesn't ask to be worshiped with all kinds of rituals. Worship him in your own Self, in your own heart." Elsewhere the Lord says, "Remaining in the heart, I enable the inner instruments of mind, *chitta*, and intellect to attend to their respective functions." You can use other terms such as *Rama, Krishna, Peter*, or *Moses* for your empirical purposes, but to experience the Self constantly, use the mantra *So'ham*.

Remove all your doubts about the mantra, and remember, it is good to repeat *Om namah Shivaya* and *Guru Om*, but your entire being is made up of *So'ham*. By remembering the mantra *So'ham* without stop, your very body will be converted into *So'ham*.

Q: I have received mantras from several Gurus, and now I am somewhat confused about which mantra to use and which Guru to follow.

Baba: A great saint, Molana Rung, told this story about a farmer digging wells in his field. The farmer dug down fifty feet but struck no water. He dug fifty feet in another spot, and he couldn't find water there either. He dug in a third spot and still didn't have any luck. So he dug a fourth well and started digging a fifth, but I am afraid he won't find water in the fifth well either because this farmer's problem is that he doesn't dig deep enough. If instead of digging five wells he had dug just one a hundred feet deep, he would have found water and would have spared himself a lot of trouble and money. When you receive a mantra, you have to give your heart and not hold it back. Just as you took a mantra away with you each time, you also took away your heart—as when you play with a child sometimes by showing him a chocolate and taking it back again. What you should do now is decide on one mantra and repeat it. With its help, try to go deep within yourself.

Q: When I repeat the mantra, sometimes it stops and my mind begins to roam among external things.

Baba: In those things too you should see the object of the mantra. Continue saying *Om namah Shivaya* to whatever your mind rests on. Regard everything as Shiva. A great Siddha has said that the ornaments may be many but they are all made of the same gold. Identify with the gold, not the particular form of the ornament. Repeat the mantra with the same view. Meditate. It will not take long for you to grasp the reality.

Q: What is the importance of chanting?

Baba: The divine name has enormous importance. From my earliest life I have been fond of holding week-long chants and singing the divine name. As a result my ferry reached the other shore while I saw the boats of many great Vedantins getting sunk midway.

Tukaram Maharaj talks about chanting with great truth. He declares that the power of his chanting is so glorious that by means of it he will make the mouth water of one who pours out philosophy, as one's mouth waters upon seeing another eat sweet candies. By chanting Rama Krishna Hari, he'll bring yogis out of *samadhi* and make them dance to the tune of his chant. By the power of the name he'll turn this very world into a most glorious heaven, compared to which even Vaikuntha and Mt. Kailash will fade into insignificance. While chanting, you should consider meditation secondary. If you are chanting in right earnest, meditation will chase after you. Why should you chase after it? Meditation is the reward of chanting the divine name and reciting holy texts.

Swadhyaya, or chanting, is a powerful bath for the inner Self, the inner organs, and the mind. A person may be beautiful and wear expensive clothes, but if he hasn't had a bath, his body will give out a terrible odor. Likewise, however much you eat or drink, in whatever style you live, if your mind is not pure, what possible radiance can there be in your life? If your mind stinks, then you may use the most delicate perfumes on the outer body, and other people may delight in their fragrance, but not you. You will only breathe the smell of your own mind.

A session of chanting may last for an hour or an hour and a quarter. During that time you train yourself to master at least one sitting posture and to achieve concentration. Then there is a technique called *tratak*—gazing fixedly at an object—which is used to still thought waves arising in the mind. This is achieved by holding your chanting book at a certain distance in a certain position. I ask people again and again not to be lax in the matter of holding their books. You must hold the book straight up before your eyes. In doing so you are practicing *tratak* in the most natural manner because your eyes are fixed on the words of the text all the time. Therefore, while practicing *swadhyaya*, you are also practicing *tratak*; you are perfecting a sitting posture, and *pranayam*, or breathing, comes naturally. Your inner spirit receives the nourishment it needs, and the mind also becomes more focused.

There is a certain *mudra* in yoga by means of which all the openings in the face are closed: the ears by putting fingers in them, the eyes by placing fingers above them, the nostrils, the mouth. It is called *sharmukhi mudra*, possessing six aspects for the six openings of the face. But through *swadhyaya* you practice a *mudra* which is even more effective than the *sharmukhi* and even more purifying. When you hold the book firmly, your hands are engaged. With your eyes you read the words of the text. With your ears you hear the sound of the text, and with your lips you chant the text. In this way the mind focuses easily and naturally. As your eyes concentrate on the text, you pass mentally from one word to another and listen constantly to the sound of the chanting. This is a most mysterious yoga.

Experiences of a Siddha

It is the custom in India, when we hear of a great saint, to approach him and serve him while doing our best to take in his highest teachings. During my lifetime I have met more than sixty great saints, most of whom are no longer living, and I learned many valuable things from them. In addition to intellectual learning, which alone would not have satisfied me, I received a great deal of practical wisdom. I tested each and every inch of the whole system. In doing so, I received a lot more from within than from outside in the world. I learned of the many divine places within the body and plunged into them deeply. I learned that among the different centers of the body the richest and most complex is the heart center which resembles a lotus with sixteen petals, each possessing a particular quality. I tasted each and every quality of those sixteen petals.

As a honey bee constantly moves about a flower, so the individual soul moves about the different petals of the heart lotus, absorbing and identifying itself with the qualities of whatever petal it alights on. You can even taste these petals from afar although their actual nature will elude you until you have seen them directly within you.

Suppose you think about someone, perhaps even fall in love with him or her. Yet a few minutes later, without knowing why, you get angry. Then the anger dissolves, and you start to feel afraid. The fear is replaced by greed and then, after awhile, by excruciating inner pain. You become preoccupied with harmful deeds you may have done, and their memory haunts you. Suddenly, for no reason, you forget all this, and a feeling of peace comes over you, and then disgust at whatever you see. The next thing you know, you want to drop everything and go away. These changes are due to the peculiarity of each and every petal in the heart.

Wherever your soul alights, it drinks in the nature of that petal and identifies with it until it has experienced all but four petals which face downward. These elude it for a long time; yet if you were to become established in the first of the lower petals, you would become steadfast, immovable. You wouldn't keep changing your clothes, your job, your emotions. If you identified with the second of the four petals, you would become a great poet. Upon entering the third petal through deep meditation, you would visualize the entire cosmos. With the fourth petal, you would be filled with knowledge and universal love. It is the peculiarity of yogis who are mature in their spiritual practice to remain constantly in the fourth petal, reveling in its experience of divine love and wisdom. This lotus is common to both men and women.

I spent a lot of time in meditation, analyzing the different petals of the heart lotus. From it, I received steadfastness and the power to remain still for a long time. I learned to enter permanently the petal which gives the experience of divine wisdom and love.

One can enter the heart lotus and even learn to control the mind and stay there for a long time, but that is not sufficient. We have to learn how to become anchored in the four downward-facing petals. Only then can we experience complete freedom. When you reach that space, you are not afflicted by the pains, sorrows, and pleasures of the physical body. The pleasure of sense objects is like a shadow cast by the petal of love. We think pleasures come to us from the objects themselves, but that is wrong. When we eat or drink, we glimpse the inner joy, but the glimpse is more fleeting than a lightning bolt. If we could reach the petal of knowledge and love, we would experience joy, not only during joyful moments, but also during painful moments.

Sit quietly for a few minutes. You will experience the irrational changes of emotion and know what I am talking about. This fluttering of the soul from one center to another is caused by one's own past actions. When spiritual practice and Guru's grace enable you to enter into the four downward-facing petals, nothing in the world will be able to trap you and bind you. The fear of death will disappear; the underlying unity of all things will become manifest.

I meditated for a long time on that particular center, and now I remain steadfast there while I attend to various activities. When people come with all sorts of gifts, that's fine, and if there are no gifts, that's also fine because compared to the inner experience, material wealth is like dust.

Just by looking at a picture of my Baba Nityananda you can see that he was firmly established in the center petals of the lotus. You can see that his eyes, though they are open, are actually turned within.

Within everyone there is a divine effulgence—the Blue Pearl, or *neel bindu*, which everyone should see. After you have seen it, you become steady and tranquil. Our outward beauty and our spiritual beauty derive from its existence. When it leaves us, we are carried away and thrown into a cemetery. Because of it, we are able to love each other; man is able to love woman. There is so much love in this light. It contains no maleness, no femaleness, for it is the same in both men and women. There is no East or West in it either, no Christianity, no Hinduism, no Islam. That light is pure blue consciousness. No religion, faith, or race can reach it. It is the God who transcends all religions, and it is intensely beautiful. When you see it in meditation, you are speechless. Whatever we do is done simply to see it. After I saw the blue inner light, I was cured of my religious, racial, and national beliefs because I could see the same light in others too, and I could see that all these religious and racial distinctions were artificial. In that light they don't exist.

When, through the grace of Nityananda Baba, I saw the light of pure consciousness, it settled in my eyes and transformed them. This light is known as the lotion which enables blind eyes to see for the first time. Kabir sings of this lotion: "Since I applied the lotion of my Guru's grace, all that I can see is Rama, Rama, Rama everywhere." Tukaram also says, "The lotion of the blue light of consciousness was applied to my eyes, and their vision expanded. I overcame the figments of dual, nondual, heaven, hell, man, woman, high, low. My sense of difference was annihilated. I could see only the *atman* everywhere, and I knew that the world had never been, that, in fact, there is no such thing as phenomena. What appears to be world is in fact ParaBrahma, the supreme being. I became aware of *So'ham*, I am that, I am God."

A saint named Hazrat Basjid Bastami was a great meditator. One day as he was sitting in meditation, he began to shout, "I am the light of the world, I am the light of the world, there is no one higher than me, there is no one higher than me, I am everything, I am all, I am everything."

While he was shouting, his followers sitting outside heard him and said, "Oh, oh, Hazrat seems to have lost his mind." What Hazrat was shouting went totally against the teachings of the Muslim scriptures. After a while Hazrat came out of his meditation with a calm mind and walked outside. His followers surrounded him and said, "Hazratja, what you said in meditation wasn't true. You have committed a sin against the holy scriptures."

"Why? What was I saying?" Hazrat asked.

"You were blabbering, 'I am God, I am God, I am the light of all. There is nothing higher than me. Everything derives life from me.' "

"Was I saying that? Well, if this kind of thing happens again, you had better take some action against me."

His followers agreed. Four days later Hazrat again began to shout at the top of his lungs, "I am God, I am God. The sun functions by me. The world is run by me, the world is run by me." His students rushed to grab whatever weapons they could lay their hands on. One grabbed a rock, another a club, a third some sharp, pointed iron instruments, and they all got ready to attack Hazrat when he came out of his room. After his meditation was over, Hazrat came outside, and they all began to beat him. Bigots who haven't learned anything from their religions tend to do this sort of thing. Hazrat's students hit him so hard that he sat down and

fell into deep meditation, exclaiming, "I am God, I am light, I am the *atman*, I am the Self, I am God, I am light, I am the Self."

And then a most wonderful thing happened. The students found that their blows recoiled upon themselves multiplied ten times. For every blow they gave, they received ten blows in return until all of them were babbling idiots. At last, to save their own lives, they stopped beating him. When he came out of meditation, they showed him their broken limbs, and Hazrat said, "Hey, what happened?"

They answered, "We struck you but only hit ourselves."

"Why did you strike me?" he asked.

"You were saying, 'I am everything, all this is me, I am the Self within everyone.' "

"That's why you received your own blows back again," Hazrat answered, "because it's true, I am each one of you. If that were not so, then you would not have hit yourselves upon hitting me. All that you see is nothing but the light of Mohammed which is glorious, created by God. My heart is the very mirror of the light of God."

This is the new lotion which is applied to your eyes. No matter what religion a Siddha comes from—whether he has been a Sufi, a Muslim, or a Hindu—he is in the same state which transcends all man-made traditions and religions.

The freedom of a Siddha is such that he doesn't have to depend on others, even for his outer needs. Leave the question of food aside. All creatures eat food; birds, animals, insects, even germs eat food, and so does man. There's nothing great about getting food; what is great is the state of Siddhahood. Sai Baba of Shirdi, Zipruanna, and Nityananda Baba were great Siddhas. Food and money used to lie around them in heaps; yet in their hearts it had no value. Devotees used to come to Shirdi Sai Baba with their pockets full of money, hoping that he would ask them for it. But Sai Baba would ignore them and then perhaps pick out someone else and take money from him.

The hall where Nityananda Baba used to sit was always filled with rich gifts. Yet all he wore was a loincloth or a shawl sometimes. It is the destiny which matters, and a Siddha functions according to his destiny.

I'll tell you the story of a Siddha named Amritrai because anyone who went to see him was filled with the savor of *amrit*, which means nectar. He always sat on a silver throne and wore a gold-embroidered turban. His robes were rich and regal, and he sat majestically while people came to be in his presence for a while.

No matter where a *sadhu*, or holy man, is, all sorts of characters come to see him. Some are just curious. Others are on the lookout to commit petty thefts and pick pockets. Still others come simply for fun. Nonetheless, a few came to Amritrai to understand their own Selves. A Siddha is a pure being, full of renunciation which drips from his heart all the time. Even in the midst of treasures and wealth, a Siddha holds the sword of renunciation right before him. To a Siddha the senses have no value whatsoever. Only the supreme inner reality has value.

Amritrai was a great poet, and one day he was singing a song he had composed: "Possessions are dust, they are ephemeral. What intelligent man would seek them out?" While sitting on a silver throne, wrapped in sumptuous robes, he sang, "Who will chase after fleeting possessions, why build these enormous palaces? A humble hut is so much better. What need is there for majestic royal robes? It is better to sew patches of cloth together and make a covering for your body." Amritrai sang, "I feel like begging crumbs from house to house," while, in fact, he was eating from plates of gold.

One learned man in the audience stood up and said, "What on earth are you talking about?"

"Why are you angry? What I am saying is absolutely true," Amritrai replied.

The man snapped back at him, "It's all right for you to talk about renunciation while you sit on a silver throne and wear royal robes and eat from gold plates."

"Oh, learned sir, what am I to do?" Amrit said, "My *karma* torments me; it will not leave me alone!"

"Is that so?" the man answered. "In that case, why don't we meet here tomorrow and go for a walk in the forest?"

The next day Amritrai accompanied him. The scholar found a secluded corner of the forest where there was a hut. He asked Amrit to sit in front of the hut and not to move from the spot.

"I am going to beg alms now. Please stay here until I come back."

On the other side of the forest lived a king who was a disciple of Amritrai's, for Amrit was the Guru of kings. Often devout kings make a vow not to eat until food has first been offered to fire and some guest has been fed. This day too the king commanded his soldiers to look for a *sadhu* to be his guest for lunch. The soldiers galloped through the forest until they came across Amritrai sitting in front of a poor hut. They asked if he would come with them to have lunch with the king. When Amrit arrived at the royal camp, the king recognized him and gave him his throne to sit on. It was lunchtime; so food was offered him on the king's gold plates.

Meanwhile, the scholar had managed to get a few crumbs of bread and was bringing them back to the Guru when he passed the king's camp and saw Amritrai sitting on the throne, eating from gold plates. When Amrit saw the scholar, he shouted, "Oh, learned sir, see how my *karma* torments me, deliver me from it."

A Siddha has enormous power. I used to visit Zipruanna and always found him naked. Dozens of dogs and pigs would be around him while he sat peacefully in their midst. In India it is a tradition that you never go empty-handed to visit a saint but always bring fruit or candy or some other gift. Whatever Zipruanna received, he would throw to the dogs and pigs who ate it. Sometimes when I came to visit him, he would grab my wallet, pull all my money out, and throw it to the animals. Sometimes there would be as much as one hundred dollars.

"What makes you think that dogs and pigs eat money?" I asked.

He snapped back, "Is it proper for a man to eat what even dogs don't eat?"

That was the kind of being he was. He reclined on a pile of filth; yet he had great power, for that was his destiny. Bhartruhari, the great poet-saint, sings, "It is impossible to say a word about the ways of perfected beings or to know anything at all about their *karma*." Some live completely naked, lying on the earth without even a torn piece of mattress, and some live in splendor which outshines even that of kings. Some are serene and calm; others are mute all the time; still others never stop swearing and lie around like snakes.

If my Guru Baba Nityananda happened to lie down on one side, he would stay that way for three or four hours before turning over. A sage has said that some Siddhas act like Siddhas while others act like mad men and still others act like evil spirits. In spite of this, they are kings, not beggars.

In Nagpur there was a being named Tajuddin Baba. He was a very great saint, and kings would come from far away just to be around him. He was addicted to only one thing, and that was wandering around on foot, which he did all the time. One king presented him with a *tonga*, a horse-drawn carriage. Another king offered him a car. They brought him expensive shawls, but Tajuddin went on walking while the *tonga* and car followed behind him. He kept the shawls in a bundle slung over his shoulder and walked naked. Sometimes he dropped the bundle beside the road, and the shawls were left behind.

Siddhas behave in countless different ways. They teach scholars and learn from idiots. They fight with heroes and run away from cowards. If people give them gifts, they renounce everything, and if there is no one to give them gifts, they go begging. Those in whose heart the master of the heart has taken residence behave in contradictory ways. In the bitter cold of winter they drink cold drinks, and in the heat of summer they eat peppered foods. Such beings can do anything. What appears valuable to others is cheap to them. As the poet says, "I am not deceiving you. I am not saying a word which is untrue."

Siddhas don't have to pretend because they are saturated with divine bliss. Their senses fall slave to them; they don't fall slaves to their senses. There is no distinction for them between Self and other, between sin and virtue, between great and small. They may live like beggars, but they are not beggars; they are kings. They are the wealthiest of all beings. In fact kings come to beg of them.

A Siddha is drunk on knowledge of the spirit. This doesn't mean that he will stumble about and fall in a hole. Being drunk on knowledge, he knows *aham brahmasmi* (I am God, I am the absolute reality) while also knowing *sarvam kalvidam Brahma* (everyone is God, the same light of knowledge shines within everyone). Knowing this, he soars with intoxication. His sense organs are continually directed toward the bliss of knowledge. Indra is supposed to be the Lord of heaven. Possessing all wealth, he has the most splendid elephant, Airavat. His heaven is full of nymphs more beautiful than the most beautiful women on earth, but even Indra is a beggar compared to a Siddha, not to mention earthly kings who compared with him are as dust.

For a long time my mother wanted a child. She began to worship Shiva and chant *Om namah Shivaya* all the time. Every Monday she fasted, and she regularly gave a holy bath to the image of Shiva. Then she met a Guru who gave her *prasad* and told her to repeat a certain mantra while remembering Shiva in her heart. The Guru also told her to repeat Shiva's name all the time, before bathing, before eating, before leaving her house, before doing anything. Eventually she had a son. While feeding her son, she would repeat Shiva's name. She would grab her son's hand and ask him to repeat *Om namah Shivaya* before eating his food. As a result, I grew up to be a great devotee of Shiva.

At one time I practiced Ayurvedic medicine, but I gave it up because I realized that there were many others doing the same work and if I left it would be no loss to anyone. Then I turned to the spiritual path. Even now I occasionally recommend Ayurvedic medicine. But my principle work now is to prescribe, not for physical ailments, but for the disease of existence which is more widespread than all other diseases put together. Other diseases afflict only the sick, but this disease afflicts even healthy people.

Q: What made Swami Muktananda become a monk?

Baba: From my earliest years I had heard about saints and about God from my family at home. Then, around the age of fifteen, I happened to see a play about a young boy named Prahlada, who was a child saint. As I watched the play I was deeply moved, and soon after that I left my home, for I suddenly felt a powerful pull toward the Lord.

Q: How did Swami Muktananda know that he had become a God-realized being? What was different about the feeling before and after?

Baba: If something goes wrong inside you, you feel it immediately without anybody telling you. In the same way, if something good happens inside you, you don't need anyone's opinion to let you know about it. In your present condition, you are aware when you are happy or unhappy; likewise, when you realize God, you become aware that you have realized him. Truth has the power of making itself known to you and also of making you aware that you have known it.

Q: Were you always fond of laughter and gaiety, or did these develop after Self-realization?

Baba: Fun, laughter, and love are part of the Self. God created this universe for his enjoyment. Laughter is the best remedy to remove depression and mental dryness. Just as for normal relaxation there are games with bats and balls, or social clubs and dances, so laughter and gaiety are the playground of ascetics and meditators.

Q: I see that you have no teeth. If you're God-realized, why can't you grow back your teeth?

Baba: Don't worry, I have teeth—they are lying on a table in the next room. What makes you think a God-realized being should be a dental mechanic? Your next question ought to be, If you are a God-realized being, why do you need somebody to give you a shave? Why not dematerialize your beard? And why do you have your clothes laundered? Why can't you wash them automatically by your powers? In fact, you don't know what God-realization means. God has apparently developed a division of labor. In his world, dental mechanics make dentures. What's the point of using spiritual powers for such a trivial purpose?

Besides, the body has its own physical limitations. If you lose your teeth, why should you want them back again? Why not accept it? I can talk, explain things to you, and sing without teeth. If I wore my dentures, I would speak, talk, and sing in the same way. It's wrong to think that God exists to satisfy your trivial needs, to suppose that he will supply you with new teeth and new fingernails and cure your sore throats. The inner power obtained as a result of God-realization should be used only to help other people realize God in their turn. For a God-realized being to start materializing dentures and dematerializing illnesses would be like asking God for a pinch of tobacco instead of for title to the spiritual kingdom. The only gift a wise man asks of God is the gift of love, the gift of repose in the inner Self. And even that represents a low degree of understanding. Someone who is fully enlightened doesn't ask God for anything. He only wants to love him more and more. A true devotee doesn't do business with God. He doesn't say, "Since I am offering you devotion, in return give me some teeth."

Q: Could you shed some light on the way God-realized beings commune with one another.

Baba: They communicate with one another through spontaneous love, considering each other to be the same Self. Just as one friend approaches another in the manner of friends, in the same way a saint approaches another in the manner of saints.

The Witness of Living
and Dying

In the Gita Lord Krishna says that if one has not sought the truth and seen the divine light within himself, if one has not had a direct experience of the inner reality, life will contain only birth, old age, disease, sickness, and negativity. No matter how great a person is, no matter what his state or ability, it is difficult to escape death although he may escape the fangs of his fellow beings. Researchers concerned with death have come to discuss the question with me. They asked how they could best help a dying man. I answered that death is the most frightful time of all, and it's extremely hard to help anyone then. If you really want to help someone, you must begin when death is still far away. Death is the most important event in life. No matter what you eat and drink, or how you enjoy yourself during your lifetime, you will have to face death one day. If you are not prepared, you will find it a very frightening experience.

One day the great philosopher Solon went to meet King Karo who was tremendously wealthy and quite conceited about it. The king took Solon around his palace and showed him all his diamonds and pearls, his horses, elephants, and armory. Then he asked, "Have you ever seen a man as happy as I?"

Solon said, "I don't find any of these things around you a source of happiness. To me, only that man is happy who has learned how to die peacefully and joyfully."

Karo was not pleased by the philosopher's words and dismissed him unceremoniously. After some time Karo invaded another country and lost the battle. The proud king was captured, and his victor commanded that he be burned alive. When Karo heard this command, he remembered Solon and began to cry, "Solon! Solon! Solon!"

The victorious king was amazed to hear his enemy calling for Solon and asked, "Why are you crying out?"

Karo answered, "Once Solon said to me that only a man who knows how to die joyfully and peacefully can be truly happy, and I didn't listen to him. Now that I'm about to die a miserable death, I remember his words, and I am filled with remorse for my lack of understanding."

This had a great effect on the king, and he set Karo free, whereupon Karo rushed straight to Solon's ashram.

Therefore, as we celebrate our birthday with joy and laughter, we should also learn how to celebrate the moment of our death with the same joy and laughter. Only he can die peacefully and joyfully who, after having delved into himself by the grace of his Guru and the grace of God, has experienced his own death while still alive. Once a person rises to that stage at which he can separate himself from his body and experience himself as pure Self which is beyond the body, he can die peacefully and joyfully, and he will inherit the kingdom of joy and happiness for many lives to come. Only through knowledge of the inner reality can we find our freedom, not through any rituals or external actions.

Knowledge enables us to realize our unity with the absolute being. It is attained when, by the grace of God, we encounter our Guru and his *shakti* passes into us and causes an inner awakening. Then knowledge arises from within spontaneously, for knowledge is nothing but an answer to the questions, Who am I? Who made me? For what? From what materials? What do I have to do? In the Shiva Sutras, Lord Shiva states, "Only when man plunges within will he be able to realize who he truly is and become stabilized in his true state."

Each day we pass through the waking state; from waking we

pass into sleep, and from sleep we return to waking, and this goes on and on. There is a tremendous lesson for us to learn from this, but we do not pay attention.

One afternoon King Janaka was comfortably asleep on his royal couch. Maids were fanning him, and armed sentries were keeping guard. He dreamt that his rival, a neighboring king, invaded his kingdom, defeated him, and drove him into exile. Weary with fighting, Janaka fled his kingdom and soon began to starve. In his wanderings, he came upon a field of corn, plucked an ear, and began to eat it. Just then the owner of the field came by and saw a strange man helping himself to his corn. He took out his whip and administered two cracks to the king. The whip hurt the king badly, and all of a sudden he woke up. When he opened his eyes, he saw that the maids were fanning him and the sentries were keeping guard. But when he closed his eyes, again he saw himself in the middle of the field where he had been thrashed. He was filled with amazement.

He closed his eyes, and again the figure of the farmer with the terrible whip in his hand loomed large before him. The king leapt out of bed immediately and washed his face. Then he ordered that all the *mahatmas*, the great holy men, scientists, and philosophers of the kingdom, should be summoned. When they were assembled, he posed this question: "Tell me which is real—what I dreamt, or what I see now? When I was dreaming, none of these objects around me existed. There were no couch, no maids, and no sentries guarding me. I was thrashed by a farmer. But now I am back in the waking state, and the events of my dream no longer seem real. I see that I am quite safe in my palace. Therefore I must know: Which of these states is real?"

The holy men were puzzled and wondered how to answer the king's question. If they called the dream real, they would have to call the waking state unreal; but if they called his waking experience real, they would have to call his dream unreal. The king became enraged. "I have been feeding all these holy men for years," he shouted. "They have built huge temples, monasteries, and ashrams in my kingdom; yet they can't answer a simple question. All they've been doing is getting fat."

He ordered them all thrown into prison until further notice. Then he published in the newspapers of the realm the one question which tormented him: "Which of the two states is real? Dream or waking? Anyone who can answer this question is most welcome to come and explain it to me."

There was a young boy whose name was Ashtavakra, which means "deformed in eight places." One day he asked his mother, "Where is my father?"

She said, "He is in prison because he couldn't answer the king's question."

"Then you must send me to court so that I may answer in his place."

He was carried in a cart and brought to the palace where a large gong had been placed along with a sign which said that anybody wanting to answer the king's question should strike it. The boy began to strike the gong loudly. The palace gate was thrown open, and he was taken to the king's reception hall. The courtiers of the kingdom also took their seats. When Ashtavakra began to move in his funny, deformed way, the courtiers started laughing. They were amused that this misshapen creature should take it upon himself to answer the king's question when the learned men of the kingdom who had studied the Vedas and the priests expert in ritual were rotting away in prison.

Ashtavakra stood and waited for the laughing to stop. When it subsided, he began to laugh hilariously himself, and it was their turn to be surprised.

The king said to the boy, "These courtiers were justified in laughing at you because you walk in such a funny way and you are so young. But tell me, why are you laughing?"

Ashtavakra answered, "Your majesty, I had heard that you and your courtiers were knowledgeable people, but now I see how stupid all of you are. You cannot see beyond the body. You laugh at my deformities which are only skin deep. Your majesty, whether you consider the body of Brahma the creator or that of the tiniest insect, whether you consider a healthy body or one that is sick and deformed, it is made of the same five elements. If you were to look at me from the point of view of the Self, you would

see that the Self too is the same in everyone and that there is nothing to laugh at. Those who cannot penetrate beyond the body remain stuck there. As for your question, I will tell you: Waking is no more real than dream and no less real. When you dream, there is no waking, and when you are awake, there is no dream. Because one negates the other, neither can be true."

You can experience the divine state only if you pass beyond waking, dream, and deep sleep. If you remain on this side, it will elude you. We are not willing to find out what we really and truly are. We are more concerned to find out what other people are and what they are doing; yet only if we turn our concern inward, can we get anywhere. In the waking state we eat, drink, acquire, and possess, and we end up feeling exhausted. In deep sleep, we sink into oblivion. There is nothing more we can achieve during these two states. But the highest truth, the real Self, enjoys these three states of waking, dream, and deep sleep.

The Upanishadic seers raise a vital question: Who is the one who perceives the events of the waking state as distinct and separate from itself? Who is aware that "this is my house, my wife, my child, my husband, my friend"? Who is the one who stays awake during sleep when your physical body is idle? Who watches all the events of the dream state and reports to you on waking up, "This is what I dreamt"? The being, the Self, which perceives the activities of waking, dream, and deep sleep while remaining apart from them is the real truth. It is called Brahman, or absolute being.

Therefore you should learn to soar in the inner skies. You should learn to dive into your own Self. Only then will you realize what you really and truly are.

Ram Tirth once asked, "What is death for man?" and answered it with the following story. A black magician propitiated a certain deity and was granted a wish in return. He wished that he could multiply himself to forty identical forms wearing the same clothes, the same necktie, the same boots, and the same beard. He passed his life in a state of elation, and when his last days approached, the messenger of Yama, the God of Death, came to lead him honorably from this world. But the magician said to himself, "No one is cleverer than I. I have cheated so many all my life without being caught, why should I let the God of Death catch me now?"

When he saw Yama's messenger in the distance, he immediately turned into forty identical forms, and the poor messenger couldn't tell which one he was supposed to take. No matter how closely he looked, he couldn't quite pick out the one he had come for and had to go back empty-handed. The magician was proud of his ability to assume forty identical forms, and when he succeeded in deceiving the messenger of death, his ego inflated still more. Meanwhile, the messenger went back to Yama and complained, "I tried to get the man you asked for, but there were forty of them, and I couldn't tell one from the other."

The God of Death picked out another messenger who was much cleverer, whispered something in his ear, and asked him to go and get the magician. Again the magician saw the messenger coming and assumed his forty forms. The messenger approached. He walked along the line of forty forms and began to admire the perfect skill of their creator. "What a wonderful artist you are," he said, "to have created such magnificent forms. How much I thank you for the opportunity to witness your achievement." The magician's ego was already inflated, but now it puffed up even more. The messenger went on, "How absolutely wonderful these are, and yet there is one tiny flaw."

The magician said, "Hey, what are you talking about?"

The messenger grabbed him by the neck, "You are the one I was looking for," and he dragged him away.

The seer asked, "What is your death?" You yourself. There is nothing more treacherous than your ego. It has cheated millions of people. The inner awakened *shakti*, as it moves upward toward the highest center, consumes the very place where ego resides. When this self-sense disappears, don't think that your perception of reality becomes disrupted. On the contrary, you begin to see reality for the first time. You see that the entire cosmos is encased in blue light. It is like looking through a glass and seeing everything blue. When the Blue Pearl descends into our eyes, descends to our other sense organs, we begin to see the world constantly in blue, as full of bliss, and that is the final end of our weeping. One who can see the indwelling Lord laughs even in the hanging noose, but one who isn't able to see him weeps and cries even when smothered with cushions.

Q: Many people predict that the world is heading toward destruction.

Baba: So many predictions are made about the world that I wonder which to believe. It would be different if they all predicted the same thing. The truth is that the world has always been in turmoil. Somewhere bombs are being dropped; elsewhere there is progress. Somewhere ten are dead; elsewhere ten are born. Somewhere there is famine; elsewhere people are sick from overeating. Here people laugh with love; there they cry with pain. Some distribute bread; others beg for it. What prediction is contained in this? It happens every day.

Only one prediction is absolutely true: Good actions will bear good fruit; bad actions will have bad consequences. The great saint Tulsidas said, "O God, our nature is to err; yours is to forgive." I fully believe this. You should have more faith in the forecast that God will look after us and save us.

Q: Germany has produced many great philosophers. I am puzzled that they also produced a Hitler. How do you explain this? Why should an evil like Hitler exist?

Baba: Every protagonist has his adversary. During the time of Lord Rama it was Ravana, and during the time of Krishna, Kamsa opposed him to the end. So it is not surprising that Germany should have a Hitler to oppose the philosophers.

Lots of people like Hitler exist in this world, and a Hitler is born for them. Think for a moment. Was everything good before Hitler? There is no Hitler these days, but is the present time so much better than his? Lord Krishna says that the three gunas have their play in his world at all times. Misery and suffering never lack. "O Arjuna, you should transcend the three gunas."

Don't argue about God's creation like a lawyer, saying why did he do this or that. God's understanding is excellent. He has made everything as he thought it had to be. This sort of inquiry has nothing to do with the relationship between the Lord and the devotee although it may interest others.

A Muslim saint, Ibrahim, king of Baghdad, bought a slave. After a few days, out of sheer generosity (the king was very good), he asked his slave, "What name shall I give you?"

"Whatever you like, your majesty."

The next day the king called him again and asked, "What clothes would you like to wear?"

"Your majesty, whatever you give me I will wear with pleasure."

The third day again the king asked the slave, "What work would you like to do?"

"Your majesty, whatever you want me to do, I will do it gladly."

"What wishes do you have?"

"Your majesty, can a slave have any wishes of his own? His master's wish is his wish."

Ibrahim got down from his throne at once. He took the slave's hand and made him sit on his throne by his side and said, "I not only free you from slavery to me, but I also accept you as my Guru. I have learned a lot from you. You have taught me how to behave toward God."

It is the fashion these days to institute an inquiry into everything that happens, but don't question the ways of God. Instead look into your own actions and feelings.

I learned Vedanta from the works of Kabir Das. He used to tell funny anecdotes full of deep meaning. One day two *fakirs* were sitting under a fruit tree. They had finished eating and were smoking ganja. It was a tall tree, loaded with small round fruits. Next to the tree grew a pumpkin vine on a trellis. Its huge fruits hung down; yet the vine was ridiculously small. The fakirs each had a puff of ganja and began to feel quite brotherly toward each other. As they looked around, one said, "My dear friend, do you think God is just?"

"Of course God can never be unjust. Why do you ask?"

"You say he is not unjust, but look at that vine. It is tiny while its fruit is so big. Then look at this tree which is huge yet its fruit is so small. Is this justice?"

While he spoke, a fruit from the tree dropped on his head, and he cried, "Alas, O God, there is certainly justice in your world. If the fruit of this tree were as big as a pumpkin, it would have finished me off without doubt."

Instead of finding fault with God's ways, think about your own deeds. Only much later will you understand the logic of God's ways.

Q: Have you foreseen your own death?

Baba: You know when it is coming. You can foresee it. People like me welcome death much more than life. When you are alive, you are subjected to so much trouble; you have to eat and drink and talk endlessly. But when you die, you dissolve into pure being. A man welcomes the repose of sleep compared to the friction of waking. Similarly, a wise yogi prefers pure deathless being. A yogi may become sick of life but never of death. That is the mark of a true yogi.

The Secret of Renunciation

It is entirely true that supreme peace follows renunciation, which is the highest attainment. But renunciation is a subtle practice about which there are many misconceptions. For example, it is often thought that one has to live in a cave or a forest to attain peace, that meditation, austerities, and yoga are reserved exclusively for *sadhus* and renunciates who have relinquished their homes. But this is wrong, for yoga, meditation, and detachment are meant precisely for those to whom worldly life, business, household, and wealth are important.

Renunciation is essential, but what does it mean and how is it accomplished?

In India, many so-called perfect renunciates eat only when food is put right into their hands. A man once said to me, "Swamiji! Look what a great renunciate he is! He eats only when he is fed. A half-dozen people have to find ways to get food into his hands."

I said, "Listen, brother, I take my own food punctually without anyone's help. I have renounced the half-dozen people who are kept busy for the sake of one."

Renunciation should result from knowledge and understanding of truth. Otherwise, what's the point? One person gives up his home only to build another in an ashram or forest. One discards white cloth to wear saffron. Thus only the color of the cloth, only the outer form, has changed.

In this context, it would be useful to reflect on the example of King Sikhidhwaja whose story occurs in the *Yoga Vashishtha*. King Sikhidhwaja was a great seeker of liberation who possessed genuine curiosity for true spiritual achievement. As days passed, his aspiration became more intense. He went to meet great saints and hold *satsang* with them, and he also practiced *sadhana*. After pursuing different kinds of discipline, he decided that further progress was impossible without renunciation. So he sent for his beloved queen, Chudala, and opened his heart to her. "I cannot live without inner peace," he said. "My ignorant mind is constantly frightened of this world. The pride of 'I am a king' will not leave me; yet I sleep and eat like any human being. Why shouldn't I relinquish this perishable and fleeting life right now when after all it has to perish one day? O Queen Chudala! You are my beloved wife. Render me one service. Kindly sit on my throne and rule my kingdom so that I may be free to seek peace without distraction."

The queen knew full well what the king was going through, for she was a great yogi and had attained the knowledge of past, present, and future. She could see that the king was deluded by a wrong idea of renunciation, but merely talking about it would not do any good. With clear insight into his character, she allowed him to depart.

The king retired into the forest solitudes of the Himalayas, raised a hut in an uninhabited region, and began to perform *sadhana*, practicing meditation, mantra repetition, and austerities. But the more he followed severe restraints, the more unsteady his mind became. The truth is that a man will find peace and joy only in that way of life which corresponds to his disposition and upbringing. If he acts against his grain, he will feel unhappy no matter what he does.

The king had lived for a long time in royal grandeur, but now he wore rough bark, lived in a straw hut, and slept on a deerskin. He took cold baths and ate roots, tubers, and fruits. As a result his mind became more troubled and restless every day. Nonetheless he perservered, for he was a true seeker. He continually thought in

terms of renunciation. If peace follows renunciation, he was still
far from it, he thought. Perhaps he had not renounced enough.

Queen Chudala was a great yogini having the gift of om-
niscience. Moreover, she was a modest and faithful wife. To her,
the universe was *chiti's* outward expansion. She had a cave of
equanimity right in her palace, and she was constantly aware of
the supreme Lord while engaged in any work. Because she looked
upon all things as vibrations of *chiti*, she was a complete renunciate, in the scriptural sense of the word. She had not relinquished
her home but the sense of difference that alienates us from our
own Self. As a result, she was free from anxiety in her worldly
affairs to the extent of her inner quietude in meditation. Also the
power of yoga enabled her to travel anywhere she liked, with the
Blue Pearl as her vehicle. She could assume any physical form.
She had many times spoken to her husband about the true nature
of the inner Self, but the king had regarded her merely as a wife
and therefore had not learned from her instruction. The queen
waited patiently for the right opportunity to bring her husband
around, for it does not avail to reason with a person before his
time. Through meditation, she kept herself fully informed of the
king's condition. By means of her inner vision, she could see what
he did and what he left undone.

The king practiced renunciation more vigorously. He emaciated
his body by reducing his food to an exclusively fruit diet, taken
first, once in two days, then once in three days, and finally once in
five days. The queen felt troubled about such excesses. She could
not wait any longer. By the power of yoga, she took on a new
form and appeared to the king as a seer named Kumbha. The king
was astonished to see an unfamiliar seer. He welcomed him re-
spectfully and offered him a seat. Kumbha inquired after his condition. The king told him about his inner plight and added, "O
venerable seer! I have not obtained peace as yet. Kindly show me
some method by which I may attain it."

The seer said, "Your majesty, there is only one way to peace:
renunciation," and with that he vanished. When the king heard
this, his surprise was even greater. He began to think: "What

more can I abandon? I have discarded my throne, wealth, possessions, power, glory, comforts—in fact everything. I have given up
attachment to near and dear ones, acquaintances and friends, and
now live in a straw hut in a mountain forest. Yet the seer says,
'Renounce.' What more is left for me to abandon?"

Oppressed by doubt, he decided to give up his hut, his deerskin,
his water bowl, and even the bark he wore. After a while Kumbha
turned up again and said, "O king! Are you happy? Have you
obtained peace?"

The king replied, "Venerable seer! I am still as far away from
peace as ever. I am pining for it."

The seer said, "Your renunciation, it seems, is not complete as
yet," and vanished.

The king again brooded on what more he could abandon. He
decided to carry his renunciation to its utmost extreme and discard everything he had, even his body. He thought, "I'll build a
great fire and throw all my things into it. Then, finally, I'll
jump into it myself. When this body is consumed, I will certainly
attain peace." He collected dry logs from the forest, made a big
pyre, and lighted it. He recalled his associations with each of his
objects and put them in the fire one by one, saying, "O dear hut! I
have lived in you for many days but without peace. Now I offer
you to the fire. O dear water bowl! I drank water from you for
many days but without peace. Now I offer you to the fire." At last
all he had was on fire. Only his naked body was left. He circled
the pyre three times and then said, "O my dear body! I gave you
delectable foods to please you, but I did not find joy. I bathed you
in perfumed baths, but I did not find peace. I gave you beautiful
maidens to enjoy, but I did not obtain contentment. I washed you
and fed you and adorned you; yet I remained without tranquillity."

He was about to jump into the fire when the seer Kumbha
appeared, caught him by the hand, and said, "Wait! What is this
horrible act?"

The king replied, "O seer! Having renounced every possession,
I now relinquish my body. Surely this will bring me supreme
peace."

"O king!" Kumbha said. "If the cremation of the body could give peace, everyone would surely do it. How can you attain peace when you are burning the very body that is essential for finding it? This body of yours is made of flesh and blood. Its miraculous inner structure arises from the union of the father's sperm and the mother's ovum. What in it is specifically yours that you may abandon? O king! Man eats the food growing from the earth, spends his days on its surface, and finally merges into it. Therefore, this body is really made of earth. How can you give up the body which was given to you by others and consider it renunciation of something belonging to you? For one who has attained true knowledge by the Guru's grace, what is there to discard except the sense of 'I' and 'mine'?"

On hearing the seer's words, the king understood that he had no right to abandon the body which was not his at all but a gift from God.

In fact, the only thing we need to relinquish is *abhinivesha*, the source of all miseries, which has been defined in the scriptures as follows: "To regard as ours something that does not belong to us and to identify ourselves with that which is not the Self." Ego is responsible for reducing God to a limited, individual self, happiness to sorrow, and one to many. If ego could be replaced by *So'ham*, there would be nothing left to renounce.

The wrong kind of renunciation bestows confusion instead of peace. Renunciation can be the most entangling enjoyment while discriminate enjoyment is the highest renunciation.

I am reminded of a verse: "He who knows the Guru's lotus feet as the sole reality does not care whether the world is real or unreal." Only when the mind becomes free from argument can it perceive *chiti*'s playfulness. Then the universe is seen to be God himself.

When a seeker gives up *abhinivesha*, he sees one *chiti* flowing through sense organs, actions, and outer objects. At this stage, misery ends once and for all. He begins to look after his everyday affairs with ease, reverence, and devotion, for he sees God underlying them all.

When King Sikhidhwaja discarded *abhinivesha* according to the teaching of the seer Kumbha, his outgoing mind turned inward at once. He plunged into his inner depths until he reached the Self. He became immersed in the *samadhi* state. Aware only of oneness, he resembled an insomniac who glides into a long and profound slumber. When the mind that has been turbulent for a long time actually finds peace within, it discards mentation and becomes blissfully one with the Self. When the king's attention finally turned to the outside world, he found it pervaded by the same bliss. He began to see the opposition of solitude and society as a merry product of delusion. Now he neither preferred forests and uninhabited regions nor denounced towns and cities. Having awakened from his error, he felt an urge to return to his palace and actually did so. From then on, established in the inner Self, he ruled his kingdom and accepted gladly whatever destiny brought him. He experienced *chiti* vibrating far and near, in hunger and thirst, hope and despair, justice and injustice, contentment and avarice, anger and agitation.

Though he accepted differences for practical purposes, in his heart he was only aware of undifferentiated unity. He beheld the light of his own soul illuminating his ornaments, food and drink, wood and stone, animals, gods, human beings, sages, and seers. He perceived one God permeating this animate and inanimate universe.

Dear ones! One thing is certain: Whether you are enlightened or not, you have to bear the consequences of your past actions. An ignorant man weeps and grumbles in slavery to the differentiative mentality; a wise man sees the world as *chiti*'s sport and enjoys it innocently. Both the ignorant and the enlightened have to live their lives, but one remains engrossed in the enjoyment of outer sense objects while the other becomes one with *chiti*'s inner play. As the latter has accumulated merit through innumerable lives, he will be chased by beauty and material wealth; yet he will not be born again. Nor will he become entangled in sensuous delights. Though he appears worldly to the worldly, from the spiritual viewpoint he is a great yogi who has become one with the absolute.

Ordinary people see a cleavage between sense enjoyment and

the spiritual goal of meditation. To extinguish his craving for enjoyment, a meditator feels compelled to direct his mind toward a purely spiritual object. But the yogi who has become one with the absolute is constantly in meditation, whether bathing, eating, drinking, coming, going, dressing, or wearing ornaments. In this state, inspired by *chitshakti*, a Siddha yogi can outwardly be a king and live in splendor, be indifferent and indrawn like Jadbharat, become a naked *avadhoot* like Rishabhdeva, or behave like a mad, devilish creature. However, this is determined by destiny. Chiti may bring us honor or infamy, prosperity or adversity. We should accept all as gifts of her grace.

Truth, inner equality, awareness of the Self of all, and faith in the Guru's teaching are the best paths to fearlessness. Just as a fish remains thirsty in water, a man without Guru's grace finds this blissful world barren and savorless. He imagines a serpent in a rope and falls prey to fear.

If we could see ourselves truly, we would find that we are neither denizens of hell, animals, human beings, or gods but pure perfect souls in our innermost nature. Dwell on this thought until you imbibe it fully.

The mind stirs only as long as the world is seen to be different from the Self. This churning of the mind divorced from the Self constitutes our worldly chains or bondage. When one's own soul is perceived as pulsating in the world of the movable and the immovable, the mind discards mentation and merges in *chiti*. The person whose mind is one with *chiti* sees the Self on all sides. Then concepts of body, *maya*, duality, and distinction dissolve into the pure One, the goal of the scriptural authors, called *satchidananda*. The world is as one sees it. When the soul irradiates the eyes, the entire universe is perceived as Self. Just as at sunrise, darkness appears as light, likewise, in the dawn of self-knowledge, the world appears as Self.

Separation is at the root of all pain. Although distinctions are not real, they appear so. When the Guru's grace lifts the veil of duality, a seeker realizes God within himself. This is the state of *jivanmukti*, the state of spontaneity—a worthy destination for man. To deserve this, we must be devoted to the Guru, meditate according to his instructions, and follow the path shown by him.

Dear seekers! Equipoise is what we should possess, disharmony what we should renounce. Awareness of one life is the true nature of all. It is, indeed, the absolute. This is the message of all saints.

Q: How can I break bad habits forever?

Baba: Quite simply, by cultivating good habits. That's the purpose of renunciation. Through renunciation you can conquer anything, but you should be careful to renounce only bad habits. Don't renounce devotion, for example, but insensitivity. Don't renounce purity, but wasteful ways of living; not discipline and regularity, but lethargy and slovenliness; not traditional restraints, but modern license; not love, but malice and hostility; not awareness of your human greatness, but the mentality of self-dislike. Don't renounce inner things, but outer things.

Get drunk on the inner brandy, and throw away the outer brandy. Get high on the inner drug of *So'ham* and throw away the outer drug, for the inner drug will reveal the Lord himself. Visit inner nightclubs and see *kundalini* in all her beauty, and stop visiting outer nightclubs. Turn within. Be aware that the kingdom of God lies within your very body. I am not suggesting that the husband renounce his wife or the wife her husband. The relationship between husband and wife, between brother and sister, and between friends must not be renounced; they must be enjoyed.

Wear beautiful clothes, get a haircut, wash your body with soap of a good quality. Let God be pleased with the way you respect your body. God's lover should not look like a prisoner in a dungeon whose beard is tangled, whose hair grows wildly, and whose body emits a foul smell. Don't think that renunciation means to renounce beauty and hug ugliness. Look at me. Even though I am an old man, I am quite a dandy. The Lord dwells within your body; therefore you should keep it pure and clean and beautiful. Renounce anger, envy, jealousy, malice, hostility, impurity, and unclean habits. Instead, live joyfully through the practice of true renunciation.

Q: For the last two years I have been doing *sadhana* in solitude. Here among people, I feel scared. Should I go back to the mountains?

Baba: It is often good to stay alone. During my *sadhana* I too spent a long time alone, but it is wrong to develop distrust for people while living in solitude. You must learn to see in everyone the same Self on whom you meditated when alone. In Mecca the Muslim priests asked Rabia, "Don't you feel uneasy among so many people?"

She replied, "I do not live in the midst of people; I live in the midst of God."

Live in solitude, but don't fear and distrust others. See God in all of them. Once your fear goes, you will see only God's love. To be with people is to be in the company of God.

Q: I feel great resistance toward people and toward the Guru as well. What should I do?

Baba: Let there be resistance toward the Guru. How much are you in accord with yourself? If you are not in accord with yourself, how can you be in accord with the Guru? Only one who is his own friend can become a friend to others. Although you may feel resistance toward the Guru or toward anyone else, in reality the feeling is aimed at yourself. It is better to root out your resistance and replace it with love.

Saint Tukaram was asked, "If God offered you a wish, what would you ask for?"

He replied, "I would ask not to hate anyone but to see everyone as the same Self."

I once read about a man who said to another, "I want to dig a hole for my enemy."

The other man said, "Why not start now?" So the first man started to dig, and soon he stood waist deep in the hole. The second man remarked, "See what has happened? You dug the hole for someone else, and who knows when he will turn up. But just now you are the one who is in the hole."

We think ill of others, and who knows when that thought will reach them; meanwhile we are the ones who burn.

Q: Could you talk about *samskaras*? What are they? How are they made?

Baba: According to the scriptures, *samskaras* are the impressions or tapes which become imprinted in your psyche as a result of the deeds you have performed. These tapes are imbedded in the central nerve which we call *sushumna*. From time to time, they rise to the conscious surface and then merge into the central nerve again as you lose awareness of them. It is not easy to uncover these tapes or past impressions, but when your *kundalini* is awakened, you can perceive them arising from within very clearly. They are the leftovers of past deeds. Take the example of an infant just an hour or two old. The mother puts him on her breast, and he begins to suck like an expert. That is the result of *samskaras* which can also be called habits remaining from past lives.

In the same way, all our thoughts, as well as the meditation and chanting that we do, leave their *samskaras*, or impressions, in our psyche. That is why it is essential to stay conscious and alert. Because whatever you think or feel effects your entire body, you should strive to keep your mind empty of thoughts. But if you can't do that, then let only good thoughts move in your mind. Although your bad thoughts may be directed at others, they harm only you. In the same way, calm, loving thoughts help you while helping others too. Prahlad, a great devotee of the Lord, says to his father, "Father, know that whatever harm one thinks to inflict on others, whatever harmful acts one commits in thought or deed, leave impressions imbedded in one's own mind. Henceforth they will cause suffering, sorrow, and anxiety within oneself."

Therefore, instead of thinking and doing harm, it is better to keep thinking of the Self who lives within everyone as pure consciousness. Every thought is like a seed cast in your mind, the fruits of which you yourself will enjoy later on. That is why I stress chanting so much. Chanting destroys old *samskaras*, old tapes embedded in the mind. For not a single word you utter ever goes to waste.

Q: What do you have to say about proper diet? For example, is it wrong to eat meat?

Baba: I don't say that you mustn't eat meat, but you don't need it for meditation. In meditation, the inner energy first purifies your body. By eating meat you are making the body impure again; so there is more work for the energy to do. If you want to reach higher stages of meditation quickly, it would be better to give up meat for a while. Eat light foods that will give you strength, for example, butter, milk, and sugar. What meat do those animals eat whose flesh we eat? They are strictly vegetarian; they live on grass and leaves, so we too can get our strength and flesh through vegetarian foods. I'm not against meat eating; however, for meditation it is necessary that your food be pure. If you were to eat pure food for a while, you would get into the higher stages of meditation more quickly.

Q: What is the importance of sexual energy? Why should sex affect the *kundalini shakti* adversely any more than playing music or gardening, if one is unattached and discriminating with the action?

Baba: It is absurd to speak of remaining unattached in the sex act. The two things are at opposite poles. Nonetheless, I am not condemning sex. All I am saying is that to remain unattached to sex and to be its victim are one and the same thing. The sexual fluid is your very life, and there is nothing which *kundalini* loves more. When, by conserving sexual fluid, one becomes *urdhvareta*, one whose semen flows upward instead of downward to waste, he acquires the power of *shaktipat*, or transmitting *shakti*. Therefore you should spend sexual fluid like a miser. Don't be an enemy to your own life. A whole body is formed from one drop of sexual fluid. Therefore you must value it. The body weakens when you begin to waste your semen. Conservation of sexual fluid is ecstasy; it is joy.

Sometimes I wonder about people here in America. Many claim to be civilized and intellectually evolved; yet sex is all you seem to think about. Even birds and animals are not possessed by sex all the time.

The truth is that everybody has sexual energy. Krishna, Rama, and Buddha had sexual energy, and they had children too, but they used their sexual energy in a disciplined way. They were not possessed by a form of hopeless, chronic lust. You must have a capacity for self-control and a degree of renunciation. You must try to find out why you have been born as a human being. In what way am I different from a tree, an animal, or a bird? These are the important questions. As far as sexual energy is concerned, who doesn't have it? Who doesn't indulge in the sex act?

But there is such a thing as an appropriate time and place. For example, I am surprised at the mentality of people who, even in the presence of a saint or yogi, find that all they can talk about is their obsession with sex. This brings a story to my mind.

A shepherd named Ramja took his sheep to the forest to graze. It so happened that the king was out riding in the forest that day. It had been a long ride, and he began to feel hungry, for he had forgotten to bring a lunch. Just then he saw Ramja the shepherd among the trees and asked if he had anything to eat. The shepherd offered to share his humble meal which consisted of curds, plain *chapattis* of millet, and some gruel. Since the king was extremely hungry, he found the food delicious and enjoyed it very much. Before riding on, the king gave Ramja a letter authorizing him to come to the court and visit him any time he liked.

One day a wedding was to take place in the shepherd's family, and he had to do some shopping in the capital. While he was there, he decided to use the royal letter and pay a visit to the king, who was delighted to see him. The king gave him a meal and offered him his love. Then he said, "Ramja, what do you want? You can ask me for anything. You are my honored guest."

Ramja thought for a moment and then said, "Well, I really like to chew tobacco very much, and where I live people add slaked lime to make the tobacco taste better. Maybe you could let me have some slaked lime of a very good quality."

"You foolish man," the king cried, "you could have asked me to give you the forest in which you graze your sheep. I could have made you a great lord. Yet all you ask for is a little slaked lime."

That's what happens when you fall slave to your addictions. What's the point of going to a *sadhu*, or a holy man, and asking him for some slaked lime?

I would like to tell you another story. Two owls who were husband and wife went out hunting. When they came back, one had a serpent in his beak, and the other had a frog. The husband-owl with the serpent was about to crush it when the serpent caught sight of the frog in the wife-owl's beak and darted his head over to eat it. The serpent had forgotten that he was being crushed in the jaws of death. When the frog saw the snake, it fainted away because fear is more powerful even than death.

I have nothing against love between husband and wife. How could I? God has created men and women. Therefore he has sanctioned the marital relationship as well in all its aspects, the physical included. But you don't have to go to a saint to understand this. To what saint do owls, donkeys, and camels go? Yet they all enjoy the bliss of a physical relationship. It is a part of life, and it will always be so.

Q: If God wants me to be without sex, why did he create lust and temptation?

Baba: What makes you think that he created them for your personal use? God also created hell. Is that for your use too? He created sorrows and disease. Are they destined for your use? God also created the state which is free from lust; have you thought about that? He has created the various passions along with their consequences and this world in which you suffer them. Think it over. If God made heaven, he also made hell. Remember both. Don't go by what God has created but by what is good for you. Who created poison if not the same God who also made honey? What shall we eat, poison or honey?

Nothing but the Self

I

In the Gita I have often read, *gahana karmano gatihi,* "The ways of *karma* are unfathomable." This is true. Even great scholars have hesitated to comment on the mysterious ways of *karma.* All that can be said about the matter is contained in a verse I once read: "What has been written by destiny, according to karmic law, cannot be wiped out by anyone—Lord Vishnu, Lord Shiva, Lord Brahma, or any other god—even the Lord of Death is subject to the great force called time."

In this world Ram has gone, Krishna has gone, Buddha has gone; Jesus and Moses too have gone, and Nityananda has departed. Who then will be the exception? Who has come here to live forever? People arrive in the world, spend some time here, and they go. It is not a great thing. If the feeling "I am Brahman, I am Shiva, I am the Self, I am love, I am consciousness" arises in your heart, if your devotion to the Guru is real and your love is real, what harm can there be?

You ought to grasp my teaching fully. Knowledge of the Guru does not only mean to consider his body as the Guru and to weep and worry about his bodily presence but also to become firm in the inner understanding and knowledge of the Self which has been given by him.

I have taught *So'ham.* I have taught "I am the Self." I have taught "I am consciousness." I have also taught "I am different from the body, and I am the witness of the body." When a person breaks the law, he may be sentenced to four months' imprisonment. If he undergoes the punishment peacefully, his sentence will be reduced, and he may come out after three months. On the other hand, if he acts up in jail and protests too much, his punishment may be extended from four months to four years or maybe to fifteen years. That is how we reap the consequences of our actions. Pain and pleasure do not come from anyone else; they come from ourselves. Pleasure and pain are nothing but God who is truth, eternal, omnipresent, within me and within you. Within the Lord's all-pervasiveness, you are free. Act well and you go to heaven. Act badly and you go to hell. God does not interfere with anyone's *karma*. He is unattached. He does nothing. He is not the doer; we are the doers. Therefore people should think again and yet again about the sorts of actions they do. A farmer reaps the fruit of what he sows. If he sows bad seed, there is no point in crying when the time comes to eat it. The seers have called this world *karma loka*, the world of action, because man enjoys the fruits of his acts here. If one performs acts conducive to liberation, such as meditation, then he is liberated. Truly speaking, everything we do, we do for ourselves.

Remember, the body is perishable no matter to whom it belongs. In the Gita the Lord says, "This world is evanescent and ephemeral. This body is only temporary." Eternality is only in the Self. The Self alone is worth attaining and worth seeing. The Self alone is worth befriending. How beautiful my Guru, Nityananda Baba, was. His body was so lovely. Yet he too departed and Muktananda will depart. The entire world will depart. But first there is one thing you must do, and that is to attain the Self.

The fruit of thought is very great. In the end, according to the Gita, you attain what you think about all the time. Therefore, whatever else you do, sit calmly and contemplate the inner truth that you are the Self. Just as an engineer knows himself as an engineer, a lawyer as a lawyer, and a cook as a cook, all of you should know, I am the Self, I am consciousness, I am perfect. The body is only an outer layer superimposed on consciousness. Not knowing this, we see the body and suffer its ills; yet the body too is consciousness. The entire universe is consciousness. Just as water alone solidifies into ice and becomes hard, so consciousness alone becomes manifold. It becomes men and women, good and evil. It alone becomes anxiety, love, agitation, peace. It alone becomes *samadhi*; it alone becomes fickleness. Everything is a modification of the Self. If you see yourself as the light of the supreme being, you will be filled with joy and bliss. How can you be guilty? Who gave you this wrong idea? I'm simply astonished. Only a donkey is born from a donkey, never a horse. Only a cow is born from a cow, never an elephant. Then how did you, O man, who have come from the supreme Lord, become a sinner? Once when I was in Bombay, I heard some children singing a song from a movie. It went, "The earth, the sun, and the sky haven't changed. How is it that you have changed, O man?" When I heard the children singing, a wave of understanding filled my mind. We who are the supreme Self have become individual souls. This is our only hell; we ought to get out of it this minute! And there is only one way to do it. Right now, this very instant, beat the drum of *Shivo'ham*, and sing out *So'ham So'ham*: I am that, I am consciousness, I am Brahman. Jump and dance without caring about anything else. Dance with only one idea, "I am the Self," and the Self will reveal itself to you, O man! Your wrong idea hides the Self which is manifest, eternal, and always revealed. It sees beautiful forms with your eyes, hears melodious sounds with your ears, speaks and sings with your tongue, gives and takes with your hands. In spite of this you have turned it all around and thought badly of your Self which is good, an embodiment of wisdom.

The Self is already attained. See how beautiful it is from within, how pure. What delight! It is the Self that is man, the Self that is woman. It is the Self that is the universe.

If you build a playground and carve a dog, a horse, an elephant, a camel, and a fish out of stone, do you forget that they are stone, whatever individual form they have? In the same way, you are consciousness. The horse is consciousness. Man is consciousness.

Woman is consciousness. If you become absorbed in this awareness, even for a moment, you will be extremely joyful, and then
you will know that your *tapasya*, your penance, has borne its
fruit.

When you sit for meditation, do not think of your neighbor as a
man. Consider him to be the Self. Consider him to be consciousness. Consider whatever sounds arise as the voice of consciousness. Consider all *kriyas* as movements of consciousness. See
whatever happens as consciousness. If you do this, you will be in
heaven in a moment.

It is said in the Upanishads that a wise man is never unhappy
because he knows that the *atman* is different from the body;
among temporary things, it is eternal. As for you and me, we
should meditate on the Self who, though residing in the body, is
different from the body; though residing in the eyes, is different
from the eyes; though residing in the ears, is different from the
ears; though residing in the tongue, is different from the tongue.
One who knows the Self this way never suffers, even in great hard-
ship or calamity. We have a human body for the purpose of seeing
this *atman*. Although a great and divine soul resides in the body,
we do not know it, for the Self can only be known by one who
meditates and turns his awareness inward.

Man looks at his hair, his clothes, and his polished shoes and
understands himself to be those things. He makes a great mistake
in not looking at his inner Self. One Shiva Sutra says, *Rango
antaratma*, the inner Self is the stage. The *atman* himself becomes
the stage on which he likes to manifest the drama of the universe.
The inner Self is the place where he stages the scenes in which he
wears strange and various costumes. He assumes limitations of his
own will and enacts different plays. The small and the great are all
his forms. Sometimes the mind runs after this object and sometimes after that. If you were to steady the mind in your inner Self,
Hai, Hai, in a moment, you would become God! In a moment you
would become immortal! The Shiva Sutras say that when your
intellect becomes pure and clean you find that attainment of the
highest reality had been there all along. The Shiva Sutras also say,

Dhivashat satvamsiddhi, with purified intellect we see the Self subtly and profoundly in its form as the world-drama.

Thinking of the outer world, man spoils his mind. No wonder his intellect is destroyed. He seems unable to turn his mind toward his inner Self. What *karma!* Why did God turn the intellect outward? If he had turned it inward, it would have been so good. In Rudra-tapani Upanishad it is said, *Rudra naro Uma nari.* It is Lord Shiva who acts as man and his Shakti Uma as woman. I bow down to both of them. Similarly, it is Lord Shiva who acts as Vishnu, and his *shakti* as Lakshmi. I bow down to both. It is Lord Shiva who is the day and Uma who is the night, and both of them play as day and night. Lord Shiva became the fire ritual, and Uma became the fire pit. Lord Shiva is fire, and Uma is the offering. If you could understand this, how happy you could be.

Without knowledge, man can never be happy. People may think that great power can make a man happy, but I know the condition of a man of power. People may think that earning a lot of money can make a man happy, but I know the condition of the lords of wealth. The happy person is one who has placed Rama in his heart, who performs his daily task, lives with everyone equally, and is a friend to all. In truth, friendship is the greatest thing to earn. I don't know why countries manufacture atom bombs, sowing destruction and destroying friendship. One man should be a friend to another. Our Vedas say, "Give with faith, give with respect, give with love, and give with an embrace. Give to one, falling at his feet." But see what's happening in the world. There is no safety; destruction is everywhere. How can man progress and be happy? We should look upon it as God's play. Therefore, attain the inner Self quickly, for it is said, *Siddha svatantra bhavaha,* a Siddha is supremely free.

II

Knowledge is infinite, without bounds. Therefore the quantity of knowledge you receive depends on how limited or expanded you are, and this knowledge shapes itself to your needs. One of the most distinguished of the many saints India has produced, Jnaneshwar, who was supremely enlightened, says in a verse of his poetry, "Why don't you enjoy the state in which the mind completely extinguishes itself? When the mind dissolves, the Self arises."

The most important question raised in Vedantic philosophy is, Can you attain what you don't already have, or do you attain what preexists within you? If you are to get something you didn't have before, what good will it do you? If you lacked it before, there is every possibility that you'll lose it again sometime. As for getting what you already have, that's nonsense, isn't it?

Yet that is what happens. We spend our time getting what we already have and getting rid of what we never had. This is Vedantic philosophy in its subtlest and highest form.

A great philosopher-sage in our country, Shankaracharya, says in a Sanskrit verse, "The Self, or soul, is always present, it has always been there, it will always be there. Don't think that you got it just a while ago or that you will get it after you have done some spiritual practices."

One day a woman was bathing in her tub. While she washed, a procession passed by on the road below her window. The moment this woman heard the music, she got out of her tub, dressed herself, put on all of her make-up, and came out to watch the procession. There were many beautiful young women in the procession wearing lovely rings, bracelets, and necklaces. When the woman saw this, she felt for her own diamond necklace and was shocked to find it wasn't there. "Help, help, my necklace has been stolen!" she began to scream.

Women from the neighborhood rushed to help. They looked for the necklace all over the place but couldn't find it. Then one clever woman asked her, "Where did you last see the necklace?"

"It was around my neck," the woman said, feeling her neck and exclaiming, "Look, here it is. It was hidden under my sweater."

The fact is that the necklace had never been lost and it was never found, but a false outcry was raised—my self-esteem is lost, my necklace is lost. And then, a squeal of delight—it has been found, it has been found. The necklace was never lost.

A poet-saint ways, "O man, look within, and you will see the
light of the Self reflected through the intellect." Compared to this
understanding, all spiritual practices are futile and secondary.

A king called Janaka used to sit on the bank of a river every
day and practice awareness of the inner Self, continually repeating
So'ham, So'ham, So'ham. There was also a great sage named
Ashtavakra who, though he was just a young boy, was fully enlightened. Ashtavakra happened to pass by the spot where Janaka
sat repeating *So'ham, So'ham, So'ham*. He sat down in front of the
king, holding his water bowl in one hand and in the other a
yogdanda, a T-shaped stick which yogis use to lean on, and he
began to do his own mantra. But his mantra was not *So'ham* or
Om or *Om Namah Shivaya* or *Radhe-Krishna*. He began to repeat, "This is my water bowl, this is my yoga stick, this is my
water bowl, this is my yoga stick."

The king opened his eyes and saw a nuisance sitting right in
front of him in flesh and blood. He said to himself, "I am trying to
contemplate God, and here is a fellow who comes and starts in-
dulging in his own brand of *japa* [mantra repetition]. I left the
capital behind and sought this solitary spot to get away from
noise and disturbances, but they seem to be chasing after me, even
here."

When Ashtavakra saw that the king was getting upset, he began
to shout even louder, "This is my water bowl, this is my yoga
stick, this is my water bowl, this is my yoga stick." Finally,
Janaka became so angry that he stopped doing his *japa* and said,
"O brother, what are you doing?"

The boy said, "You royal ass, what are *you* doing?"

"I am doing *So'ham, So'ham, So'ham*," the king answered.

"I am also uttering a truth," replied Ashtavakra. "This really is
my water bowl and my yoga stick."

Janaka the king said, "You holy ass, who says the water bowl is
not yours? Why do you have to shout at the top of your lungs?"

Ashtavakra snapped back, "O king, I am a young boy, so I can
be forgiven if I'm a little less intelligent, but you are supposed to
be subtle, enlightened. Who has told you that you are not *that*,

that you are not *So'ham*, that you are not the highest truth? So what's the need of repeating it like a moron?"

Immediately the veil lifted. The king got up, hugged the boy, and said, "You haven't been a nuisance at all. On the contrary, you have done me the greatest kindness."

Manpuri says that the Lord is within your body yet you wander from place to place in search of him. It's like somebody holding a child in his lap yet sending a town crier around to announce that the child has been lost.

An ecstatic saint, Mansur Mastana, used to soar in the inner spaces where he saw the highest truth, crying, "*Analhaq, analhaq,* I am God, I am God, I am in the midst of truth, and the truth is in my midst." He began to dance, "I have found it, I have found it." The orthodox clerics, who never understand a thing, accused him of uttering blasphemous heresy, and Mansur said, "I do not mean to utter heresy. I am only speaking the truth which I have experienced directly." He continued, "You may break a mosque, you may break a temple, you may break any other holy place, but you must not break the human heart because there the Lord himself dwells. Inside a temple you worship an idol, inside a mosque you worship nothing, but in the temple of the heart the divine light sparkles all the time. That is the true house of the Lord."

Because he said this, he was hanged, and he proclaimed the same truth even from the hanging noose, "Down with all priests, down with all scriptures. Fling them into water; proclaim fearlessly, I am God, I am God, I am God! Mansur Mastana says this: I have recognized my true master in my own heart."

III

The Yoga Vasishtha contains a great doctrine: The world is as you see it. The two terms are *drishti* and *shristi*. *Drishti* means all that exists; *shristi* means your own eyes, your own perception. Whether you suffer loss or gain, happiness or sorrow, whether your heart leaps or goes dead, it is all your own creation; nobody else is responsible. One creates one's own joy, one's own suffering, one's own *karma*, but we hold other factors responsible such as country or government or destiny or parents. We become friends with one and sway in the joy of that friendship; we become hostile to another and reject his presence. Yet it is we who have created friend and enemy alike. Therefore, change your eyes, make them divine, and you will see the world as it really is.

Swami Ram Tirth was a great Vedantic philosopher and one of the first Indian saints to visit America. One night he was watching the beauty of the sea and swaying in that beauty. Close to him slept a man who suddenly began to cry, "Save me, save me, chase him away." The man woke up and asked Ram Tirth, "What happened to that three-horned tiger?"

"I didn't even see a one-horned tiger. I have been sitting here quietly. You saw the tiger and now you are asking me about it."

That is our condition. We create our dreams, and then we ask others about them; yet they are all figments. All man's creativity, his scholarship and learning, his pride of understanding, are products of dream perception, not true waking perception. We see our own projections, our own attitudes; we become enmeshed in misery which is our own creation, and then we cry out.

Swami Ram Tirth told a story about a man who went into a palace of mirrors. He looked up and saw his reflection; he looked in front of him, and there was his reflection again; he looked to the left and down below, and then he sat quietly, feeling exalted: "Oh, there are so many of me." After sitting for a while, he came out. In the meantime a dog got in. As he rushed about the palace, he saw a number of dogs coming at him from the opposite direction. He turned, and again there were fifty dogs rushing at him and barking. The dog became terrified. Alone, surrounded by a thousand enemies, he barked and barked and leapt and leapt until his heart failed from sheer fright and rage, and he collapsed. Rage and fear are the mantra of heart failure.

Shaivite philosophy calls this universe the dance of *samviti*, the play of creation, and it is like a palace of mirrors. One who sees *samviti*, or consciousness, in it becomes liberated. But one who sees his own projections as the dog saw his reflections in the mirror and thought they were his enemies dies in sheer misery.

Through meditation we should earn eyes by which to see our own Self in everyone, for the sense of other is the root of our fear and the cause of all evils for us.

In Yoga Vasishtha there is a story which illustrates how we see our own projections in the world and respond to them. A king was so stingy that he had become known as the king of miserliness. An actor came to his kingdom to present a play, and for several months the actor performed at the royal theater. But since the king was such a miser, the actor never got even a dime from him. By this time all the actor's own money was gone, and he was beginning to get discouraged. So one night he announced in public that this was going to be his last performance. The evening began, and the actor performed with great enthusiasm. The play went on and on. Soon it was 3 A.M., and still the king hadn't parted with a cent. By now the actor's wife had given up all hope of receiving anything from the king. In an hour it would be broad daylight. What could they expect from that royal miser? So she began to slack off in her performance. When the actor saw this, he recited a verse to encourage her, saying, "A long time has passed already, not much time is left. Don't slacken now, a few more hours and we will be done."

An ascetic was sitting in the audience. When he heard the actor's words, he picked up his only blanket and threw it at the actor. The princess sat in the audience too, wearing a rich necklace. Upon hearing the words she took it off and threw it toward the actor. The prince sitting next to her wore a jeweled ring. He took it off and threw it on the stage too. And then the show ended.

The king was enraged that his son and daughter should part with such valuable jewelry. Although he had given nothing, he couldn't bear to think that anyone else had given.

"O Babaji," he shouted to the ascetic, "you only have one blanket. What made you give it to the actor?"

"Your majesty," the ascetic said, "I have been watching this show for a whole month. I have seen the splendor of your court and the power that you wield, and I started to feel that maybe I had been wasting my time going on pilgrimages, fasting, and remaining celibate. My body has dried up, and nothing has come into my hands. I decided to stop all these practices and to change my life so that one day I could become a king like you, enjoying splendor and power. At that moment I heard the actor's words, 'A long time has already passed, not much time is left,' and suddenly I realized that most of my life has already gone by, only a short time is left. What point could there be to changing my style of life now? It would be so much better to go on doing as I have done. This realization filled me with such happiness that I threw my blanket at him out of sheer gratitude."

The king then called his daughter and said, "What about you? What made you throw your precious necklace to the actor?"

"Father," the princess said, "I have come of age as you know and am in the halo of my youth. By now you ought to have found a prince for me to marry, but you're so miserly you haven't even thought about it. So I decided to elope with the son of a rich man. Then I heard the actor's verse this evening, and I thought, 'I have already waited for so many years. You are an old man, you will probably die soon. Why should I elope now and spoil the name of our family?' Out of sheer gratitude I threw my necklace to the actor."

Then the king asked his son, "What about your ring?"

The prince said, "When a son comes of age, his father ought to vacate the throne in his favor and do *tapasya* in solitude. But you are so greedy that you hang on to your power even though you are almost senile and can't sit properly. I'd been conspiring lately about ways to bring you down from your throne. When I heard the actor's words, I thought, 'So much time has already passed. You are so old. Why should I commit a crime against my father?' In sheer gratitude I threw the actor my ring."

Only one sentence was spoken; yet three hearers heard different things according to their own situation.

In a similar way, three leaders once went to the Guru Prajapati. They were the leader of gods, the leader of demons, and the leader of mankind. All that Prajapati said to them was, "Da, da, da," the same word three times to all three. When Indra, the leader of gods, heard Prajapati's word, he construed it to mean, "Control your senses," for he knew that the gods yearned for sense gratification. In fact, that was their only pursuit, for heaven is not a land of *tapasya* but a land of enjoyment. On the other hand, Virochana, the leader of demons, took the word *da* to mean, "Have compassion," because he knew that demons were brutal creatures, plundering and burning people in cold blood. This being the case, what they needed most, he felt, was compassion. When the leader of men heard the word, he recalled how greedy and avaricious men are, how they spend their time trying to earn more and more money. So he construed the word *da* to mean, "Give." In India ever since, there has been a long tradition of giving in charity. Only one word was used; yet three meanings were heard, inspiring three kinds of action.

That is exactly what happens to us. Our eyes have become a trap, creating a world in which we are not free. Yet one who can see this world as the sport of *samviti*, the dance of consciousness, sees neither man or woman, sin or virtue, high or low, but only the same dance in everything.

The analogy of the snake and the rope is used quite often in Vedanta. A man out walking one night sees a piece of rope lying on the sidewalk and thinks it's a snake. He starts to yell and people come running to help him. Someone, reaching into a tree for a branch, grabs a snake instead and dies of its bite. Finally the people get a light and discover that the snake was only a piece of rope but that the branch had really been a snake. They grumble at the man, "If you had only been aware that this piece of rope was not a snake, then your fear would have vanished, and our towns-man would now be alive."

Meanwhile another townsman says, "This is not a piece of rope at all but a wavy pattern made by water; erase it and the fear will go."

And the third townsman says, "No, it's a crack in the earth; if you fill it in, there will be nothing to fear."

Those who came to eradicate fear created new misunderstand-ings. Because we don't understand what things really are, we cry for help, and people come with lights, and they don't understand either.

The truth is that the same *chiti kundalini*, or consciousness, appears as the universe, just as the rope appears to be a snake.

Because we don't see this, endless numbers of thoughts arise entrapping us in ourselves. We analyze our thoughts and struggle to find a way out, and suffer, and find ourselves more deeply enmeshed. Just as the rope appears as a snake, so knowledge appears as ignorance and causes us pain.

Through meditation we overcome the illusion of a serpent, ridding ourselves of bondage and limitation. When a great sage saw this truth, he spoke to God, saying, "O Lord, what is there that you are not? You are man, woman, son, and daughter; you are virgin, and you are married. You become an old man and walk with a stick, and you are yourself the stick."

If through daily meditation we saw God's light sparkling within, the veil would be drawn aside, and we would be able to see creation as it really is. As we meditate more and more, the divine conscious light comes into our eyes. Our eyes see the same light outside us, and we know the universe to be nothing but that light.

IV

Jnaneshwar Maharaj tells of a man who wanted to see the clay from which a pot was made. He crushed the pot into powder, mixed water with it, and transformed it to a lump of clay. Yet it was clay even before he did all this. Jnaneshwar says, "Why couldn't you see the clay even in the form of a pot?"

In the same way people recommend a form of meditation in which we absorb the body into the *prana*, or vital force, the vital force into the mind, the mind into the Self. Having attained the Self, we are supposed to know and experience peace. Why take all this trouble?

Other people ask us to concentrate on the space between the eyebrows in order to get into meditation. Still others ask us to concentrate on the ears. There are so many techniques, but Lord Shiva says, "Why can't you recognize the truth in all these created objects without picking them apart?" One who achieves this recognition immediately experiences the bliss of the Self called the bliss of *lokananda samadhi sukham,* the bliss of the universe as it is. Because we don't recognize this truth, we go to a great deal of trouble meditating and engaging in various activities. Not that I'm against meditation. Indeed I myself ask you to meditate, but why do all these things? Because we have not experienced the omnipresence of Lord Shiva. The moment we do, the truth of the Self appears to us.

The Shiva Sutras were inscribed by Lord Shiva himself with his trident on a rock. *Chaitanyamatma,* the *atman* is consciousness, states the first Sutra. In my commentary on this Sutra I have written, "In all places, things, and times, the *atman* is ever the same. He lives in all and is yet different from all. He is with everyone and yet the friend of no one . . . when a fire flares up, sparks leap of their own accord and fall back into the fire. In the same way, countless universes arise and subside in the *atman* by themselves. Amid the appearance and disappearance of universes, the *atman* remains utterly tranquil and immutable. He is the highest bliss, the indweller."

The *atman* is already an embodiment of purity. What can there be to purify? Knowing this, one can experience the Self immediately.

A saint, a simple and good soul, was approached by a disciple named Svetaketu, who asked to receive his teachings. The saint answered, "Oh, Svetaketu, what am I to tell you? Everything is only the Self; just as water solidifies and becomes ice, so the very same Self appears as this universe. Know this and you will know everything." Svetaketu bowed down to the master and went away. But he didn't understand what had been said to him. He reflected, "What did the Guru say? Everything is the Self? What kind of instruction is that? Shouldn't he have asked me to do Hatha Yoga or *pranayama,* or to shave my head or to grow a beard, or to concentrate on this or that? Instead, he simply asked me to reflect on the Self."

If one has a keen intellect and the power of discrimination, what kinds of practice are needed to recognize the truth which already exists in the form of the Self? How long does it take to recognize the inner principle? Only a fraction of a second. It's so simple. On the other hand, without the power of understanding, many lifetimes would not be enough. Lord Rama once asked his Guru, "Oh, Lord, how long does it take to experience the Self?"

His Guru answered, "O Rama, it doesn't take this long," snapping his fingers. Yet ages have passed and people have not recognized it. It is so easy, yet so difficult. Nonetheless, for one who is simple-hearted, truthful, devoted to the Guru, for one who has unwavering faith in God, a snap of the fingers is long enough.

In his dissatisfaction, Svetaketu approached a new Guru and asked again for instruction. This Guru told him he would have to wait for twelve years while he served the ashram in one capacity or another. Svetaketu agreed, and the Guru asked his secretary, "What kind of job is there for this seeker?" The only vacancy left was a job picking up buffalo dung. Svetaketu was sincere and true, and he never hesitated about the nature of the work. He was willing to spend twelve years and more if that's what was needed to receive his Guru's wisdom.

One day, twelve years later, he looked at the calendar and found out that he worked two days more than twelve years. He went to the Guru and said, "I have finished my twelve years of service."

The Guru said, "Now I will tell you what you need to know. It is this: The Self alone appears in all things. You, too, are the very same Self. Know this and you will know everything."

Svetaketu said, "O Guru, I already had this instruction. It's nothing new to me. Why did I have to pick up buffalo dung for twelve years?" "It is due to your own foolishness," his Guru replied.

Therefore, our meditation should be *lokananda samadhi sukham*, the bliss of recognizing the eminence of the Lord in everyone. All that we see is made of the supreme Lord. The Shiva Sutras state, "The Self is the dancer in all these forms." In the Vedas it is written, "Because we see duality in others, we are afraid." Fear is the recognition of duality. We are tormented by others only because we see the otherness in them. I read a poem in

Marathi which states, "Man becomes his own enemy; for there is no outward enemy. He alone creates wrong notions for himself."

When a beautiful sculpture in the shape of a god is set up, people rush to worship it. Yet all along they had their own Self which is pure consciousness. I don't understand this sort of mentality. Keep your mind permanently immersed in the idea, "I am Shiva, *Shivoham*, I am that, *So'ham*, I am the Guru, *Guru Om*." Whatever taste or preference you have, try to identify yourself through that taste or preference with the reality from which all things arise. All the divine beings worship one who entertains this notion without stop. During my Baba's time, many gods and goddesses used to sit in the trees near the ashram. Therefore, constantly repeat *Shivo'ham*, *Shivo'ham*, I am Shiva, I am Shiva. By dwelling on the surface you have forgotten the real truth. You are satisfied to repeat the idea, I am guilty, I am guilty, going to bed with it and rising with it in the morning. Why not go to sleep with this idea: I am Shiva, I am Shiva. At the very beginning of the Upanishads it is said, "Oh, mind, constantly think well of yourself. The distinction of man or woman exists only in the outer sheath. The Shiva dwelling within is the same in all."

Afterword

by Shankar

I

A BIOGRAPHICAL SKETCH

Swami Muktananda Paramahansa (Baba) was born in South India on May 16, 1908. He left home at the age of fifteen after a normal childhood in which he showed marked qualities of intelligence and an independent character. Even in India where it is not unusual for a boy to leave home in quest of spiritual knowledge, fifteen is precocious. Muktananda pursued his quest throughout India, visiting many ashrams and holy places. He spent an extended period at the ashram of the great Siddharudda Swami where he was initiated into *sanyass*, the order of orange-clad monks. It was then that he received the title *swami* and his name, Muktananda, which means "bliss of freedom." The young swami was said to be obsessed with the desire to attain the state of *mukti*, or liberation.

In the end, he did attain that high state but only after many years of exacting spiritual practice. His search for the right teaching did not bear early fruit. True, he mastered many of the yogic arts; he became an expert Hatha yogi and a fine Rajah yogi. He learned agriculture and cooking. He studied the abstruse yogic philosophies—Vedanta and Shaivism. He mastered the scriptures. But all this learning did not give liberation. Instead, his burden and sense of urgency increased year by year.

During his wanderings he met sixty of India's greatest saints, including Zipruanna and Hari Giri Baba. These were men and women of fully realized consciousness. Each had something to teach, but none could offer Muktananda the inner completion for which he strove. Finally, in 1947, just past his thirty-ninth birthday, Muktananda came into the presence of the great Siddha, Swami Nityananda of Ganeshpuri. Nityananda was a remarkable being. Austere, wholly detached, he overwhelmed everyone who came before him. Muktananda was no different. He became like a child in front of the saint, and on the day of India's independence, August 15, 1947, he received initiation by *shaktipat diksha* from Nityananda. The loincloth-clad Nityananda transmitted his spiritual force into Muktananda by eye contact and initiated the final spiritual unfolding. This phase lasted for the next nine years. During that time Muktananda underwent a thorough transformation. He had many spiritual experiences, an amazingly candid account of which he has given in his spiritual autobiography *Play of Consciousness*. These experiences culminated in 1956 with his attaining Self-realization, liberation or Siddhahood. Muktananda had been raised by the compassion of his Guru to his Guru's level. He now had the power to help others in the same way.

In 1961 Nityananda's life came to an end. Muktananda, established in his ashram in Ganeshpuri near Bombay, now stood at the head of the Siddha line. The whole world was his ministry, but it was not until 1970, after years of preparation, that he first visited the West. Again in 1974 he returned and this time has had a decisive influence on American seekers of inner unfoldment. He has initiated thousands by *shaktipat* and contributed to establishing a genuine spirituality in the West. The public portion of his mission is only just the beginning.

II

DISCIPLESHIP AND FREEDOM

People are wary of exploitation. Whatever their theoretical objections to the institution of the Guru, an overriding concern is fear of domination by another mind and another will. And it cannot be denied that lesser Gurus exploit in ways that can be simple (money, sex) or complex (psychological and psychic power games). The Sadguru, however, is not an exploiter. If we look at all our relationships objectively, we will find that they are all exploitative to some degree. We use one another for comfort and security if not for more gross purposes. Only the relationship with the Sadguru is not based on need and insecurity but constantly renews itself without constraint.

The Sadguru is simply living his life freely and happily, communing inwardly with God, his inner self. People come to him because they love to see, sporting with God, a being who does not involve himself with the needs and barter of conventional relationships.

The Sadguru likes us to be free too. That way we can be part of his play and not make the constant demand that he enter an attached relationship with us. Instead we can enjoy freely in his company the sport of God without jamming it up with self-concern and terror. It is in the Sadguru's interest for us to become free. That is all he cares about; all he wants from us is our own freedom. He does not ask us to become like him (except in his freedom), for God has created many forms. Each personality, each character, is an example of perfection, and the Sadguru does not tamper with that multiplicity.

The scriptures delineate certain basic yogas: *karma yoga*, the yoga of action and service; *bhakti yoga*, the yoga of devotion; and *jnana yoga*, the yoga of knowledge (the head, the heart, and the will). When we begin our inner quest, we find that all these yogas, or disciplines, apply to us to some extent. We might lean more to one or another of them, and during different periods of our development one or more of these yogas will be emphasized. The Sadguru takes all this into account; he does not mold his disciples to some preconception. He allows their development to unfold in harmony with their nature. A Siddha's head, heart, and will are in perfect balance. Therefore, he can understand the process going on in each devotee, despite manifest differences from person to person. Baba is as at home with a university scholar as with a passionate lover of Lord Krishna. The secret of his ability to guide so many disparate types is his ability to let be, knowing that God, his inner self, leads everyone from within.

Because discipleship implies a relationship of enduring intimacy, we fear that we will lose our personal independence. But the relationship with the Guru contains this paradox: It offers us an experience of freedom, perhaps our first. Relating to the Sadguru we relate to our very Selves, and the needful clinging of our other relationships is purified. Baba's teaching exhorts us to find freedom here and now. He does not want to bind us to a long spiritual search, full of frustration and dependence on him. He wants us to be free in God right now, just as he sees we truly are:

The entire world has to depart. Yes. But before departing there is one thing you must do—and that is to attain the Self. You are the Self. The Self is yours. Live forever for your Self. You are constantly thinking about your body and identifying yourself as a man. Stop! Stop! After discarding that idea, think, "I am the Self. I am consciousness."

Right now, this very instant, start saying, Shivoham, I am Shiva; Ramo'ham, I am Ram; Guru Om, So'ham, I am that; Aham Brahmasmi, I am Brahman, I am consciousness, I am consciousness. And jump and dance without caring about anything else. Dance with only one idea—"I am the Self." Then you'll see—the Self will reveal itself.

Baba doesn't want disciples bound to him for years of dry spiritual practice. He wants free beings, celebrants of God. We are the ones who try to exploit and bind the Sadguru, not the reverse, but he is too clever for us. He dances out of our offers to relate in an attached way and sets us free. We are only afraid of our own exploitative tendencies, not his.

Baba has said that to be bound to God or Guru is to be unbound. His whole life is his service to Bhagavan Nityananda. He is absorbed in his work, and a work has been given to him which perfectly expresses his character and his unique destiny. To be separate from all other beings, to be inwardly isolated, is the opposite of freedom, for such a condition only results in the intense pain of the individual ego. Freedom is found by linking up with all beings, and the means of that is service to Guru and Self in our own way.

III

THE SIDDHA GURU

To draw close to our own nature we need the help of someone who has completed his inner journey. This is the Guru. He lives perpetually in a state of awareness beyond fears and neuroses. He moves spontaneously along the natural lines of his personality, intuitively meeting situations without prejudice.

Yogic literature says that our normal shrunken condition is the result of ignorance; it is not an essential defect of our nature. When ignorance is removed, only the Self is left which is pure light, pure consciousness. Our normal sentiment of being is hemmed in by ego, the self-sense, which has tricked us to believe in our separation from other things. Observing the impersonality and power of the universe, we feel weak and small. We are afraid, full of self-distrust and feelings of inadequacy.

The illusion of our separateness is so deeply ingrained that we haven't much chance to transcend it without the help of a Sadguru, a person who has completely surmounted his own separateness. He gives the grace to behold ourselves as one with the universe. He conquers our alienation simply by showing his perfection. The limits of impotence, gross and subtle, are severed. The world becomes light, full of humor and understanding.

The West has not yet understood the institution of the Guru. Many figures who have been in the public eye are questionable. They have never been disciples. They are only anxious to proclaim their own Guruhood. Schools and sects proliferate. We have hoards of Avatars, Second Comings, and World Saviors. It is a sad prospect, but remember, the existence of false Gurus hints that there must be a genuine article somewhere which the false ones imitate. Christ's advent was also a time of false prophets with fevered countenances proclaiming themselves in the marketplaces.

Any spiritual awakening will bring with it a strange grab bag of charlatans and deluded enthusiasts. Such a time is certainly now.

The institution of the Guru is ancient and proven. It is a pity that many have debased it. Baba has said that there is no shortage of Gurus who steal your money but rare indeed is the one who robs you of your ego. A glib tongue and slight knowledge of esoteric literature does not make a real Guru. In their disillusionment contemporary seekers have become quick to label all Gurus, the genuine master along with the charlatan, as false. It is good to be very careful in dealing with prospective spiritual teachers, but care should not become paranoia. We should be able to hear the genuine voice when it sounds.

Without the help of a real Guru we shuttle from encounter groups to swingers' clubs to psychiatrists. We take an adult education course here, a martial arts course there; we make and break relationships; we change jobs, all to no avail.

A Siddha Guru is extremely difficult to find. Meeting one is the opportunity of a lifetime. Not only is he rare, he is also an enigma. He lives beyond mental rules or formulations. He cannot be pinned down. His only consistency is an inner consistency. Meeting him, we do not know what to do with him.

A true Guru has the ability to initiate the spiritual process in the aspirant. By directly transmitting spiritual consciousness, he awakens the seeker. This process is called *shaktipat,* the descent of divine energy. It is unfamiliar in the West but well known in India and in the yogic scriptures. This is the *grace* a disciple receives from the Guru which transforms and purifies his orientation toward the world.

The true Guru has practiced the mantra to the end and now can transmit it to his student with conscious force behind it. Many Sadgurus in the past have been swamis (monks or renunciants), but at least as many have lived a normal married life. One cannot recognize a Sadguru by the outer circumstances of his life, but in all cases he will hold enormous spiritual power, the divine power of *shaktipat.* Baba has called the Guru the "grace-bestowing power of God," the human agent in our plane of existence of the transmission of grace.

By his subtle influence the Guru teaches the correct way to work without ego involvement and with nobility of purpose. He takes the hearts of his disciples and, to their amazement, pumps them full of love. He gives them the direct experience of intuitive realms of consciousness and finally helps them attain the state of *moksha*, liberation.

Everyone senses a great power coiled within him, but most of the time we don't have much hope of ever reaching it. We look in wonderment at people who seem to be fulfilling themselves—a Picasso, say, or an Einstein. We feel inferior to them, but in another way we know we are their equal. That is because we intuit our own vastness. We know that we too are rich in possibility but largely silent, unfacilitated. The Sadguru is not inhibited by social demands or by feelings of inadequacy. He offers us nothing less than the same transparent self-possession, the same ecstasy of unblocked feeling and action which is his.

The Guru is really a therapist. He has subtle means for teaching the natural flow of communication. He helps his students connect with God whom he calls the inner Self, the inner kingdom. Meditation is his easy therapy. One's attention is disengaged from the external stimuli which constantly assault it and turned in toward the Self. When attention is introverted in the meditation received from the Guru's blessing, the energy of the Self is activated. It rises through the emotions and mind which stand before it partially blocking the light.

There are Sadgurus of both sexes. In fact, several great Gurus of contemporary India have been women—the late Mother of Pondicherry and Ananda Mayi Ma who still tours India. From the highest point of view, the Guru represents a level of consciousness beyond duality, beyond male or female. When we turn inside in meditation and search our depths, we find neither maleness nor femaleness—or actually we find both.

In accordance with the traditional yogic view, Baba recognizes two forms of energy, loosely, masculine and feminine, the Shiva principle and the Shakti principle, corresponding roughly to the Yin and Yang in the Chinese tradition. There is a constant interplay between *Shiva* and *Shakti*, and both are necessary for the creation and sustenance of the universe. Baba, like Sri Ramakrishna, the nineteenth-century Siddha, is a worshiper of the Divine Mother— *Shakti* or *Kundalini*. This means that he honors and loves the manifest world. He is not the kind of yogi who seeks a retreat from actual life. He is not dualistic and life denying. God appears in the world as the Shakti principle. Thus femaleness is not other than God and not other than the Guru.

A Siddha, his body, emotions, and intellect made completely pure by the workings of the energy of the inner Self, is neither man nor woman. Male Siddhas often take on the physical characteristics of pregnant women, with large breasts and a full, round stomach. This is symbolic of their nurturing, maternal qualities. They are pregnant with *prana*, or life force, the dynamic energy that distends their bellies and makes them full. The Siddha, the Sadguru, is half-male, half-female, negative and positive, passive and active. He closes the circle of sex differences and heals in his own person the breach we feel when we yearn for a partner of the other sex to complement us.

Immersed in the highest consciousness, *sahaj samadhi,* the Guru sports in the world. For those who want to learn about themselves and to grow in an inner way, everything he does is a teaching, a physical form of higher consciousness. If we try to understand him with our intellect, we cannot. It is a grievous mistake to approach the Sadguru through the mind alone.

It is also a mistake to think of the Sadguru as an abstracted dreamer. A genuine Guru will be fully conscious of what is going on around him in ordinary reality. In fact, he will be more attentive to detail, more observant than anyone else. This is because he never drifts off into narcissistic mental processes. He remains empty, ever present, and alert. A Sadguru can be a tremendously impressive man of many worldly talents and abilities. Baba is acute in practical life. He knows agriculture, cooking, animal husbandry, business, politics, management, books, and scriptures. He knows people inside out. He is impossible to fool. He knows the ways of the world and of the spirit. Those who live near Baba feel a deep security surrounding them. His own faith in God's care and protection is transmitted to them. They feel like children protected by a great, compassionate mother.

Those who come to Baba in the correct spirit always come away with something. He does not require that they leave their normal lives to receive from him. He has deepened the emotions of intellectuals and toughened the minds of the overly emotional. He works on each devotee individually, always seeking to balance and correct, to right the distortions that have come about by reason of heredity (*karma*) or upbringing.

Culture, time, and custom are the domain of the mind. The Siddha dwells beyond the mind. That is why there are times when Baba seems like a man from another planet. We sense that although he is physically here among us he is untouched by the social and cultural tensions that affect our lives and our judgements.

Baba has drawn devotees from every level of Indian life—influential politicians, village people, traditional Hindus, Westernized, ultramodern Christian Indians. He has the same effect in America, young people sitting next to their parents and grandparents at meditation retreats, bankers sitting next to poets.

Seeing only unity everywhere, the Guru does not believe in the split between worldly life and spiritual life. He knows that spiritual life can be lived as easily in tall buildings in Manhattan as in the Himalayan peaks. There is only one consciousness, and it pervades everywhere. Normal life becomes the arena of *sadhana*; the living room carpet becomes the prayer rug; the office, the place of service to the Guru.

Spiritual life is often seen as an escape, but what can be escaped? The normal relations we have with our parents, our spouse, our children, our friends are sufficient spiritual tests. If we run from these challenges, what can we attain? To become one with the universe is to enter into the proper relationship with everything. Can we attain the inward self-possession of a Siddha if we fail in our most immediate relationships?

The student of a Siddha sees the Self everywhere and lives his ordinary life as service to God. He learns to trust his intuition and to trust that the future will work itself out. In the end he attunes his painful individuality to the larger rhythms of existence and stands free, fulfilled, and happy in the midst of his normal activities.

When everyone whom we have ever met has loved us only in a conditional way, can we learn to accept unconditional love? Can we believe easily that the Guru loves us despite the erratic quality of our mind and despite bursts of anger and jealousy, the self-serving emotions that continually assault us? Faced with such a love, we feel guilty and inadequate. What have we done to be loved in this way? But his gift is unconditional. In fact, we have done nothing to deserve it. To experience this is humbling and exalting at the same time. One who has basked in the Sadguru's grace knows that it is like nothing else, a sort of miracle almost beyond comprehension.

The Siddha Guru enters us in the form of consciousness by means of his mantra (word), thought, touch, or look and creates a revolution in our being like a depth charge. His fertility is such that the slightest contact often becomes a turning point in a life.

A Siddha's actions are not motivated in the ordinary way. They are spontaneous expressions of the joyful sport of pure consciousness, without purpose or design. When Baba moves among meditators and bestows his touch, he is governed by the inner impulse that comes to him from the Self. His touch opens people and takes them into deep meditation.

There are many spiritual paths. All the popular magazines advertize Hatha Yoga, Buddhist meditation, dietary regimes, various therapies and trainings, exercise, massage, acupuncture. These paths can purify the body and strengthen the mind to varying degrees. And perhaps they can discover and relieve emotional knots, releasing psychic energy for nonneurotic uses. But, finally, they are only preparations for real *sadhana* under the guidance of a Sadguru. This *sadhana* alone leads one to the final state of God-consciousness and total spontaneity, the state of beatitude.

The Guru is not really an individual. His body is a physical form of *shakti*, or energy. When we are initiated, the Guru's conscious energy enters us and works from within. We undergo an automatic yogic process that takes different forms in different seekers. Sometimes physical movements occur, as well as internal lights, sounds, and the experience of new understanding.

The key to this process is the ever-strengthening bond with the Guru. The more the meditator feels his link with his Guru, the more fully are the energies of meditation released within him. But in the course of *sadhana* many mental impurities are uncovered, and these will sometimes cause the disciple's trust to waver. Occasionally he may think he sees faults in the Guru. What he is really seeing are the limits of his own self-trust, his mental bondage. When the seeker is critical of the Guru, his experience of unfoldment stops, and only when he works himself back into a proper receptiveness, will it resume. To criticize a Siddha is a waste of intelligence, but even that does not really end the flow of grace. The scriptures say that even the enemies of a Siddha are liberated as he defeats them.

I have seen Baba beat people; I have seen him scold beggars and children. I have seen him ignore apparently loving devotees for long periods. Who can sit in judgement on the behavior of a Siddha? Sometimes the Guru will use such means to force the disciple to an important crisis in understanding that speeds up his development. Seekers who have been abused by Baba report that their experience was filled with gratitude and new understanding.

IV

MEDITATION

Animals have a genetic health and balance that a man often lacks. They are very much in touch with their environment. They don't get in their own way with negative, self-conscious thoughts. Our mind has put us out of touch with ourselves, and the way back is entirely bound up with the health of the mind. The answer lies in meditation.

In meditation we go beneath the accidental circumstances of

our daily existence, behind our personalities and our life-dramas, to the simple sense of being which is the foundation of our personality. It is a strong place, unmoved by concern for what others think or say, oblivious to questions of status, sex, disease, wealth, or power.

At this level there is no problem of communication because there is only one here—pure being, the primal person. There is no insecurity, no desire. When we look among the objects of the outer world, we are entranced by the illusion of sensory satisfaction. Strictly speaking, it isn't the objects themselves we want— money, power, status—but the inner feelings of pleasure or security that they bring. This is obvious, but our bias in favor of externality is overwhelming.

If the inner feeling is what we really want, then what we need is a way to experience it directly without depending on outer objects. Dealings in the outer world are unpredictable. We can never be sure that we will acquire what we want. Meditation is the sure way into the realm of those feelings. It depends only on our decision to turn the mind in, and whatever is achieved in meditation can never be taken away.

The Self is one, the personalities many. As we have grown away from our instincts into our rational minds, we have lost our center of gravity. All the foundation virtues—self-confidence, self-esteem, feelings of love and strength, capacity to understand— arise in the Self. Relationship and communication are perfect there and increasingly less perfect as we are removed from there. Meditation is nothing else than a plunge into this world of inward power.

Everyone knows his own Self. It is there during all the adventures of life as the element behind the change which gives a sense of continuity. It takes only a slight mental operation to meditate on the Self. With regular meditation we become inwardly whole. Our lives work better because our point of view is improved. It's better to see a football game from the fifty-yard line than from an end-zone seat. The party seems better when we are in a good mood. Similarly the world takes on the coloring of our sensibility which meditation integrates and deepens.

Approaching meditation for the first time, people imagine there is one right way to do it, and they want a complete formula in order not to make a mistake. But approaching your inner Self is something you know about better than anyone else. There is no formula for romance in the outer world. Some court with flowers and gifts, others with sweet words, others with aloofness, wit, fervor, style, simplicity. It is the same when we draw near the Self. Our own feelings are our best guide.

V

GOD IN THE WORLD

Our normal lives often seem to lack a spiritual dimension. At times this feeling of lack is so great that we think heroic measures must be taken to overcome it. We think, for example, we have to rush to India and sit in a cave, but if we sold all our possessions and left our families a hundred times, we would not be closer to God. It's more likely that we'd be further away.

The circumstances of our life are the outer environment. Our bodies are the nearer environment. Just as it is not necessary to torture and kill the body to find God, it is also not necessary to destroy the outer body, the conditions of our present life. A realized being can work blissfully in a factory.

The Siddha sees the world as God's sport. If that is the goal, it is easy to understand that world-loathing and world-denying movements are away from the truth, not toward it. White clothes and long beards do not make a yogi. One who has retreated to meditate will always have to test his realization in the turmoil of normal life. The real yogi sees God in Wall Street, in Harlem, in city, town, and suburb. God is not in Tibet; he is inside you.

Ordinary life is a spiritual affair, full of challenges, tests, opportunities for growth. It is to be met head-on, not avoided. Among outer things the Guru is most worth having. That is because he is not really an outer thing at all. He is the inner Self manifested visibly for easy relationship. Coming across a true Guru, or even reading about him responsively, means that you have reached an advanced state.

The Sadguru lives permanently in the highest state of truth. He accomplishes all outer actions with a sense of detachment, enjoying in them the fullness of the Self. He transmits to a disciple the highest conscious energy in the universe.

Sometimes we know things intuitively, in a flash. This represents a higher form of knowledge than our normal mental experience which is verbal and slow. Similarly we receive musical shape and form, coloring and pattern, without a single verbal thought.

Higher than this intuitive realm is the realm of absolute consciousness, *chiti*. All knowledge is simultaneously present in this realm. The energy of consciousness transmitted by the Sadguru comes from this high level. It penetrates the seeker and cleanses him of mental impurities, gradually cutting through his negative emotions, his bodily weaknesses, and his wrong ideas and leading him to full absorption in consciousness itself. This *chitshakti* is the primal energy, the very source that playfully creates the universe out of her own fullness in free will.

If you spend time around Baba or read his written works, you will become familiar with the language and ideas of Kashmir Shaivism, one of the philosophies of India. Baba has found this a useful vehicle for conveying his teachings to the world, but Baba is not a philosopher in our sense of the term. In the West a philosopher proposes metaphysical systems. Philosophy, for us, is a kind of art, working with ideas and their relationship. A metaphysical system is not reality itself but a set of ideas about reality.

Baba is a Guru, not a philosopher. The Guru takes as his field of operation the real and actual. He does not care about ideas for their own sake. He tries to point his students to the reality which exists apart from any words. He may use words to help in the pointing, but his interest is practical and not intellectual. Baba's use of Kashmir Shaivism, then, is not properly philosophical. He uses the concepts in that system as a way of directing people in their *sadhana*. He does not care about demonstrating principles or theories. He takes them ready-made and tells us to put them into use in our actual lives. Baba doesn't argue about the nature of

God and Self; he doesn't demonstrate that they are one. He *sees* everything as God, and we can see that he does. He is his own lesson when he says, "See everything as God! Do it! Don't merely talk and think about it, do it!"

All high philosophies have some truth in them. Baba leans more toward Kashmir Shaivism than, for instance, toward Vedanta to clothe his thought, but that does not mean that Vedanta is less true.

To understand the difference in attitude implied by Kashmir Shaivism and Vedanta, think of the room in which you are sitting. It is a permanent structure—four walls, a ceiling, and a floor. This permanent structure which remains the same no matter what kind of furniture or event takes place in it we can call the Self. It is the permanent substratum underlying whatever goes on in the room. The space inside the room is used in various ways. Sometimes a chair is removed; sometimes one is added. Different people come and go. Now it is a place to read a book; tomorrow there will be a party. This is normal reality, the world of ever-changing and fluid events. It can also be called *maya*.

The Vedanta Guru tells you that the room is the only reality because it is permanent. Ignore what takes place inside the room, he says, because it is transitory, untrue. Vedanta therefore can be life denying in its impact. It seeks transcendence, "getting out" of life. This is a possible attitude, but it is not to Baba's taste, nor is it likely to make sense to the Western mind. Baba, like the Shaivite, says, "Consider the events inside the room to be part of the room. They too are real. The room takes these different shapes." What we call the world is really the Self appearing as the world. There are not two elements, one to be avoided. There is only the Self taking many forms. Baba accepts the reality and divinity of the world as it is and urges us to see that divinity as the very fabric of the world. We don't have to search for some obscure substratum of reality. What you see is real. In Australia, Baba was asked how to see God in a tree. He replied that God is not hiding in the tree. He is not in the tree in some way if we could only see him. He is in the tree *as* the tree.

In his commentary on the Shiva Sutras, Baba has written:

Chiti (consciousness, the Self) is supremely free. She is self-revealing. She is the only cause of the creation, sustenance and dissolution of the universe. The prime cause of everything, She is also the means to highest bliss. All forms, all places and all instants of time are manifested from Her.

Desiring to create . . . She manifests differences in Her being, appearing in countless forms and shapes. In man this conscious spirit becomes the gross, subtle, causal, and supracausal bodies. She expresses Herself as pleasure and pain, happiness and sorrow, fear, disease and agitation, as childhood and youth; as heaven and hell. Creating all things, She infuses them with Her spirit. Though Chiti becomes the universe in this manner, still She does not discard Her transcendent aspect under which She remains exactly the same—full of light, pure and untainted. She is pure awareness. Living in and as the universe, She is also apart from it as its eternal witness.

Siddha Meditation 66–67

The room and all the events and furniture within it are of one eternal substance. *Maya* is not an inferior, ignorant mistake. *Maya* is God himself. Baba uses the language of Shaivism because it appeals to his own life-affirming sense of pleasure with the creation. This world is not a test and a captivity for Baba. It is an arena of God's benevolence and a complex enjoyment of the Lord's fertile artistry.

VI

SHAKTIPAT AND SIDDHA SADHANA

Once a seeker has received the grace of a Siddha Guru, the process of his *sadhana* unfolds. In some cases the process is so subtle that it goes on beneath the seeker's awareness for quite some time. But one thing is certain: The grace of a Siddha is always effective. Once awakened, the inner *shakti* never becomes totally dormant again; from then on it steadily works for the betterment of the aspirant.

So it is important that someone who has received *shaktipat* initiation continue his spiritual practice—meditation and repetition of the mantra—with constancy. He should feel that he has received a unique blessing and should advance on the spiritual path with enthusiasm and trust in the outcome.

One should meditate every day in the same spot. It would even be good if he could have a special set of clothes that he uses only for meditation. When a place has been used frequently for meditation, it becomes easy for meditation to take place there. But more important than place is regularity. If one is unable to have a place reserved for the practice, a seeker should not hesitate to meditate anywhere with complete trust in the penetration and unfolding of *shaktipat*.

Shaktipat diksha is an ancient tradition and is detailed in the Indian scriptures.

Whatever the path chosen and discipline selected for the seeker, no real sadhana begins till a relation is established between him and the Guru. And this relation starts from the moment an inner connection is made between the two as a result of something from the consciousness of the Guru entering into the being of the disciple. This entry of the Guru into the disciple is aptly described as the impact or descent of the higher Power, the Conscious-Power of the Guru or of the very Divine through him: Shaktipat. Where this Shaktipat is not, says the Sastra, there is no fulfillment.

M. P. Pandit from *Studies in the Tantras and the Veda*

Baba is the first to bring information on this mysterious process to the West. He may also be the first Guru with the power of *shaktipat* to travel in the Western world. In his works he details the various remarkable *kriyas*, or yogic movements, that happen to a seeker blessed with *shaktipat*.

Shaktipat is transmitted through the *prana* which may be close to what Bergson called élan vital. According to yogic philosophy, *prana* is the dynamic element that leaves an organism when it dies.

Even beginning meditators experience *prana*. It is common for a meditator to feel pressure in his head as though he were wearing a hat. Sometimes he feels vibrations in different areas of the body, sometimes shocklike feelings. Sometimes his head is heavy, and he feels like sleeping. All of these are common experiences of *prana*. You don't have to have *shaktipat* to be familiar with pranic movements. If you come across an old friend, you get a rush of delight. If you see a tough-looking man on a deserted street, you get a rush of fear. These "rushes," like all emotional and psychic movements, are pranic in nature. Even thoughts are pranic movements.

Through *shaktipat* the *prana* is quieted, purified, and made steady. In practice this means that thoughts calm down, emotions become less turbulent. All the areas of subtle life become balanced and healthy. Siddha Yoga is, in the final analysis, a kind of body alchemy in which the distortions of the system are righted by the health-giving influence of the Guru's *prana*.

Looked at from another point of view, *skaktipat* is a kind of contagion like a contact high. A bouyant person makes us happy; a sad person makes us sad. Our environment is critical to the way we feel, and we react to this in our lives when we select favorite colors for our apartments or wear clothes designed to create psychological effects. Just so, the Sadguru's superconscious state raises his disciple. He does not allow himself to be brought down by his disciples' impurities. Instead he takes them to himself. The stronger mind wins. In due course he turns the disciple into a Guru.

The intensity of inner experiences varies. Sometimes the meditator may feel only the most tenuous link with the Guru. It is particularly during such times that he learns to appreciate the mantra he has received. The repetition of the *shakti*-imbued mantra ties the aspirant immediately and closely to the Guru. Feeling estranged and alienated, the seeker need merely repeat the mantra to himself, and the Guru is his. Since it is always at hand for use, the Siddha mantra is a great boon.

Baba emphasizes the power of words. Among words none is more powerful or more purifying than God's name. The mantra is fully charged with spiritual force, and if we trust in its power, we can feel its effect instantaneously. The meditator should find a way for the mantra to work for him. He should feel that the Guru is working within him in the form of the mantra. His impurities are being burned away by the mantra; his divinity is being tapped. His heart is being opened, his intellect deepened. He is linked inextricably to the Guru. The mantra tells him he is one with the

Self. He is utterly free, creative, unlimited. Such an attitude of trust makes mantra repetition extremely effective and pleasurable. One repetition with faith and understanding is worth hundreds of parrotlike, mechanical repetitions.

The heart of the Siddha path is meditation. In meditation the mind, instead of being extroverted as it normally is, is turned inside. The energy that usually passes to the outer world through our sense organs remains within and works to enhance us. The energy in both cases is the same divine *kundalini* energy. There is but one energy in man, and in most people it only works in ordinary ways—to conduct the affairs of life. In those who have been awakened by the Sadguru, however, it works inwardly and on a much larger scale.

The highest kind of meditation involves completely silencing the mind. The introverted mind rests in the Self and is quiet. It draws strength from that deep and stable place and reawakens to the outer world refreshed and powerful. We can never overestimate the beneficial effects of meditation, simple as the process is. Every desired object of life is more easily attained by turning the mind inward than by pursuing it in the outer world. A mind made strong by meditation becomes firm as a rock. It becomes clear, simple, and straightforward.

Our bias in favor of manipulating the outer world has made us feel helpless in regard to our own consciousness and often helpless even in regard to influencing the outer world. A meditator loses the paralytic feeling of helplessness. He learns beyond any doubt that by healthy thinking and proper mental discipline he can create a reality proper to him. He enjoys the play of forces in life and becomes unafraid of change.

The seeker should meditate in any way that works for him. Some temperaments enjoy meditation on the formless or impersonal aspect of God. Others find that they need a form, a personal God, on whom to meditate. Whatever method that calms and quiets should be used, and this will vary with different people. A great deal of energy is wasted on theological debate. God hasn't created a maze or a puzzle for us to solve. He is not out to trick us. In whatever way we try to reach him, he will respond with joy and rush to meet us. He does not care which school of thought we espouse, to which religion we belong, but it is essential that we meditate on him in some way.

Baba advises seekers to cultivate the habit of seeing everything as *chiti*, as consciousness. This approach is to be taken even when not sitting in formal meditation. Everything that arises in consciousness is to be regarded as a form of the divine, the play of *chiti*. Many internal movements take place in meditation. These should be considered movements of the goddess Chiti, benevolent maneuvers of the Guru's broom as he sweeps clean the murky places that obscure the light of the Self. God is everywhere and in everything. Therefore, how can we avoid meditating? What mental state is not meditation? What thought or event or object is not God?

VII

IN THE COMPANY OF A SAINT

The atmosphere surrounding a Siddha is powerfully charged—a heightened reality. Because the Siddha's attention is wholly absorbed in the present moment, everyone around him is also forced to be wholly present. In the company of a Siddha, you are not likely to wonder about the weather.

The ashram of a Siddha is pervaded by his spiritual energy. Such places are spiritual dynamos. They are experienced like ovens by people who can intuit spiritual vibrations. Although it is true that everything is made of consciousness, it is also true that there are different densities of consciousness. The highest frequency vibrates in a Siddha's home.

A Siddha's ashram is like a larger body for him. It is fully sanctioned by the great line of Siddhas and flourishes under their protection and bounty. More is to be gained and, perhaps, more also is to be lost in such a place.

Baba has compared those who live in or visit an ashram to pregnant women. They should be careful with themselves if they want to avoid dissipating the awakened *shakti*. Many times during *sadhana*, when the ego is pushed to its limits, conflicts arise with other seekers. It is only a problem caused by the impact of new birth. The seeker should remember this even in the greatest difficulty. One way that people become purified in Siddha Yoga is through their relationships with fellow seekers. They learn to respect their own psychic identity and the identity of others. Part of the learning process includes negotiating with others about matters of psychic identity. This can give rise to jealousy, envy, and insecurity about one's relationship with Baba.

Finally, the lesson to be learned is that each person's relationship is completely unique to him and each person's function is equally unique. Our relationship must spring from within, from our inner Self. It will not be an external connection based on our mental analysis of what seems to be happening around Baba.

The fastest way to the goal of self-realization is to pay attention to the clues that come from Baba himself. Sometimes we get internal messages from the Self, sometimes only from our own mind and ego. Since it's hard to be clear about this, the Guru manifests outwardly for our benefit. By paying attention to his presence and trying to do what he wants, we penetrate our very Self. Siddha Yoga is really amazingly simple. All one has to do is follow the Guru's instruction and be sensitive to the hints he gives. Once the seeker has achieved this surrender, he begins to live in a new way, from the Self instead of the mind. The Guru is Shiva, and the seeker is Jiva; the Guru is the Self, and we are the small self, the ego. The Guru is the wish-fulfilling tree. He gives and gives. The only faith we need is the faith to receive. Not only is this true, it is simple. It is not related to the abstract Guru principle or to God but to Baba himself. Although our relationship with Baba may not be personal in a physical sense (we may, physically speaking, be far away from him), it should become truly intimate. We should feel closeness to Baba as a person even if we never say a word to him.

Our thoughts create the environment of our life. If we believe in socialism, we attract others of similar belief. If most of our mental activity has to do with spiritual life, we are sure to find ourselves surrounded by people who are spiritually inclined. This is simple common sense. Whatever our minds dwell upon affects our life outwardly. Couples who have been married for a long time often begin to look alike. If we admire someone intensely, we begin to acquire his personality traits and qualities. The law of spiritual life is that we are as our thoughts are.

That is why we fill our minds with mantra and meditation. That is why we continually turn the thought "All is *chiti*, all is God" over and over in our minds. Such a thought has the power to sweep before it all separative and self-destructive impulses. As we come to experience the all-pervasiveness of God, we slowly surrender harmful beliefs; we stop defeating ourselves.

In Siddha Yoga there is an even more effective method of meditation which is to focus on our impressions of the Guru himself. Since the Guru embodies the achievement of spiritual goals, it is easy to understand why he is a perfect meditative object. He is his knowledge, and his knowledge is himself. As we grow in devotion to the Guru, our thoughts dwell upon him naturally, just as our thoughts dwell on water when we're thirsty. We wonder what it is like to experience as he does and to be as he is. Gradually we find him on our mind all the time. This amounts to a spontaneous meditation on the Guru.

This meditation, like all yoga and meditation, seeks a single goal: to strengthen and purify the mind. People who don't meditate wonder why sometimes they are happy and other times not. They wonder why success evades them or why success, when it comes, is not satisfying. Academic education does not solve this problem of self-experience which is a problem of the mind.

Some thoughts give life; others take life away. We try to be careful about our food, but we are not careful about our subtle food—ideas, impressions, thoughts. It is a remarkable blindspot in our culture. Baba emphasizes that good thoughts bear instant fruit. Therefore all our spiritual practices, from chanting to worship of the Guru, are really worship of the mind, its care and feeding. Baba teaches that the mind is in reality very pure. It is consciousness in a contracted form—the goddess Chiti sporting in limitation. Beginning seekers commonly tend to resent their own thoughts which give so much trouble when they try to meditate. This is a mistake. We should consider our thoughts elements of the all-pervading consciousness, little pieces of God.

The reason that our mind will not stay on the mantra or on the Guru is that it has not formed the habit of concentration; it is not pure. It has indulged in undisciplined thinking for many years. Every thought has a kind of specific gravity, some pulling the mind down, others lightening it. In the course of time, regular meditation lightens the mind. Heavy self-defeating thoughts are eliminated until the steady bouyancy of "enlightenment" merges the mind in light. Understood in this way, we cannot expect to attain the Self overnight. We have to replace gross thoughts with fine ones. We have to convince our mind to give up its old habits and enjoy a more refined diet. This takes time, but it is a process that is absolutely effective. A meditator is careful about what he does with his mind and how he spends his mental energy. He starts to know himself. He makes friends with his mind.

When we sit in the presence of Muktananda, we introduce our mind to the goal of its meditation. The frequencies of all radio waves pervade our atmosphere, but only when they are focused by a proper receiver, do they become palpable to us. The Guru is God's antenna. God moves through him and becomes palpable. This is a little-known secret that is learned—along with many others—by sitting quietly with Baba.

Glossary

ASHRAM. A spiritual institution like a monastery where seekers pursue the spiritual path; the Guru's abode.

APANA. Outgoing breath.

ASANA. Posture; seat; exercise.

ATMAN. Soul; inner Self.

AVADHOOT. A great mystic-renunciate who has risen above body-consciousness, all duality and all conventional standards.

AYURVEDIC MEDICINE. (Ayurveda) The ancient Indian science of medicine and surgery.

BABA, BABAJI. Term of affection for a saint, Father.

BHAGAVAD GITA. Important Hindu scripture, a portion of the Mahabharata in which Lord Krishna instructs Arjuna in the secrets of God, universe and Self, and the different forms of Yoga.

BHAGAWAN. The Lord; a divine saint.

BRAHMANISHTHA. The Absolute Reality firmly established in Brahman.

CHAKRA. A chakra or lotus is a subtle centre of psychic energy lying in the sushumna, the central nerve, the piercing of which affords unusual powers and experiences. There are seven such chakras situated in the human body.

CHITI. Literally, consciousness or conscious energy; refers to the all-pervasive divine energy of the cosmos.

DARSHAN. Sitting with the Guru; a spiritual audience at which the Guru subtly gives his blessings. To be in the presence of a Guru is to have his *darshan*.

GUNAS. The three basic qualities of nature: *sattva*—light, balance, harmony, purity; *rajas*—activity, passion; *tamas*—inertia, ignorance, darkness.

GURU. Literally, teacher; a spiritual master or guide.

GURU OM. A mantra for meditation on the Guru.

JAPA. The spiritual practice of repeating a mantra.

KARMA. 1) (Karma Yoga) Selfless action performed as service to the Lord.

2) Action; accumulated past impressions; one's destiny as shaped by one's actions of previous lives.

3) Action, force or effect of one's accumulated past actions.

KASHMIR SHAIVISM. An Indian philosophic system which holds that the world is God.

KRIYA. Spontaneous yogic movement experienced by one who has received *shaktipat*. *Kriyas* can manifest outwardly in physical movements or inwardly as mental or emotional movements. These purify the disciple and lead ultimately to perfection.

KUNDALINI. Spiritual energy; specifically, that which is latent in each person until awakened by a Siddha Guru through *shaktipat*.

MAHABHARATA. The Hindu epic, in which Lord Krishna is the main figure and from which the Bhagavad Gita comes.

MANTRA. A spiritually charged word or phrase; a short prayer with the power to invoke God or the guru. When received from the Siddha Guru, it carries with it his power and energy and is a form of initiation by him.

MUDRA. A symbolic position of the body held for a length of time; state of consciousness; that which gives joy.

MUKTA. Liberated.

MULADHAR. The chakra at the base of the spine where Kundalini lies dormant.

NADA. The various inner musical sounds heard during advanced stages of meditation; celestial harmonies.

OM NAMAH SHIVAYA. A mantra meaning, "Om. I bow to Shiva (the inner Self).

PRANA. 1) (Prana-apana) The respiratory process with inhalation and exhalation.
2) The vital force of the body and the universe which makes everything move.
3) Incoming breath.

PRANAYAMA. Control of prana; breathing exercise.

PRASAD. Food that has been offered to God or the Guru and is then distributed to the devotees, sanctified; a gift from the Guru.

SADGURU. Literally, true Guru; a Guru who can give complete enlightenment to his disciples through *shaktipat*; the highest Guru; synonymous with Siddha Guru. The Sadguru gives not simply teachings but his own soul to his students.

SADHANA. Spiritual practice; everything that is undertaken or happens during the period of spiritual evolution; the time between initiation and final realization.

SADHU. An ascetic.

SAHAJ SAMADHI. Literally, natural *samadhi*; the highest spiritual state in which there is complete absorption in divine consciousness even while conducting the ordinary affairs of life; the state of a Siddha.

SAHASRAR. The thousand-petalled lotus in the brain, located at the crown of the head, the seat of Shiva. It is the seventh and highest psychic centre, or chakra.

SAMADHI. A superconscious state; there are several types of samadhi, but the word most usually refers to that in which the aspirant realises his absolute oneness with the Universal Spirit.

SAMSKARA. Past impression.

SATCHIDANANDA. The supreme Being with the attributes of existence, consciousness and bliss.

SHAKTI. Literally, energy; the spiritual energy felt and awakened in the presence of a Siddha; also known as *kundalini, chitshakti.* The *shakti* of a Siddha is the same as his grace.

SHAKTIPAT. Literally, descent of grace; spiritual initiation of a seeker by a Siddha Guru or Sadguru in which the Guru's spiritual energy is transmitted to the disciple; also called the awakening of *kundalini,* or receipt of Guru's grace which is the same as God's grace.

SHAKTIPAT DIKSHA. *Diksha* means initiation; same as above. In the Siddha tradition, it is done subtly by means of a look, word, touch, or thought.

SHROTRIYA. Completely versed in all the scriptures.

SIDDHA. A fully realized being; one who is supremely free.

SIDDHA GURU. Synonymous with Sadguru; a perfected being who has the power to make others like himself. He has the power of *shaktipat.*

SIDDHA LOKA. Literally, the world of the Siddhas; a subtle realm inhabited by Siddhas; the state of consciousness of the Siddhas.

SIDDHA YOGA. The yoga that takes place spontaneously by means of the grace of a Siddha Guru; Muktananda's yoga. It is the comprehensive yoga which includes all other yogas. Its goal is Self-realization.

SIDDHI. Occult or supernatural powers such as anima, the power of becoming small like an atom; garima, the power of becoming heavy like a mountain.

SO'HAM. A mantra: So'ham Sah (That) + aham (I), 'That am I'.

SRI RAM, JAY RAM, JAY JAY RAM. Term of respect. Ram—the one who revels in all hearts. Jay—Victory, Hail! Hooray for!

SUSHUMNA. The central and the most important of all the 72,000 nerve channels. It extends from the base chakra to Sahasrar, containing the different chakras. When the prana constantly flows through it one becomes enlightened.

SWADHYAYA. Study of Self; specifically study of Scriptures; chanting; repetition of a divine Name.

TANDRA. The state of high consciousness, only a little beyond that of sleep, in which one sees invisible things and comprehends incomprehensible mysteries.

TAPASYA. Penance; austere or ascetic practice; prolonged self-denial or self-mortification; spiritual endeavour.

TURIYA. Transcendental state. This is the fourth state of consciousness, beyond waking, dream and sleep, in which the true nature of reality is directly perceived.

VEDANTA. An Indian philosophic system which holds that the world is not real, only God is real.

YOGA. Literally, union; union with God or the inner Self; a method of achieving this union. The classical yogas are various paths toward self-fulfillment based on different means.